CITIZENSHIP, ENTERPRISE AND LEARNING

harmonising competing
educational agendas

CITIZENSHIP, ENTERPRISE AND LEARNING

harmonising competing educational agendas

Ross Deuchar

Trentham Books

Stoke on Trent, UK and Sterling, USA

Trentham Books Limited
Westview House   22883 Quicksilver Drive
734 London Road   Sterling
Oakhill   VA 20166-2012
Stoke on Trent   USA
Staffordshire
England ST4 5NP

© 2007 Ross Deuchar

First published 2007

British Library Cataloguing-in-Publication Data
A catalogue record for this book is available from the British
Library

ISBN-13: 978 1 85856 381 7

Cover photograph: Granville Fox

Designed and typeset by Trentham Print Design Ltd,
Chester and printed in Great Britain by Hobbs the
Printers Ltd, Hampshire.

Contents

Dedicated to Karen and Alan

Acknowledgements

To all the pupils and teachers in the schools where I gathered data and particularly to Kay Dickson and Sheila Taylor, who have given me so much inspiration.

To Gillian Klein for believing in this book and for all her support, guidance and patience.

To Douglas Weir for all of his encouragement over the years.

To Granville Fox, for taking the beautiful photograph for the front cover.

To my family for their patience and support.

Acronyms and abbreviations

BBC	British Broadcasting Corporation
CERI	Centre for Educational Research and Innovation
CBI	Confederation of British Industry
CNN	Cable News Network
DfES	Department for Education and Skills
DtS	Determined to Succeed
DUBS	Durham University Business School
EISP	Education for an Industrial Society Project
GCSE	General Certificate of Secondary Education
HMIE	Her Majesty's Inspectorate of Education
LTScotland	Learning and Teaching Scotland
MESP	Mini Enterprise in Schools Project
NfER	National Foundation for Educational Research
NQF	National Qualifications Framework
OECD	Organisation for Economic Co-operation and Development
Ofsted	Office for Standards in Education
P4-P7	Primary Four – Primary Seven
QCA	Qualifications and Curriculum Authority
S1-S6	Secondary One – Secondary Six
SCCC	Scottish Consultative Committee on the Curriculum
SCIAF	Scottish Catholic International Aid Fund
SCIP	Schools Council Industry Project
SED	Scottish Education Department
TVEI	Technical and Vocational Education Initiative
UN	United Nations
UNCED	United Nations Conference on Environment and Development

Introduction

This book appears at a time when education for citizenship is firmly on the policy agenda in Britain and across many parts of the world. It also coincides with the continued growth and development of enterprise education and increasing interest in teaching pupils about new forms of entrepreneurship that encompass a need for ethical, social and environmental sensitivity. The book aims to empower teachers and student teachers with a particular interest in citizenship and enterprise education, as well as those responsible for curriculum policy in these areas. It is also designed as a reference for academic staff in universities who are currently engaged in promoting and developing citizenship and enterprise education programmes in Initial Teacher Education.

Current and future generations of teachers and teacher educators need to embrace the opportunities offered by dovetailing citizenship and enterprise education programmes. Ultimately this will lead to a much broader agenda or a *maximal* approach. The diagram overleaf summarises the differences between narrow and broad forms of citizenship and enterprise education.

Building on previous models by Richardson (1996), Davies *et al* (2001) and Osler and Starkey (2002), the right hand side of the diagram shows how we prepare pupils to become enterprising citizens in the 21st century. Democracy and communitarianism, two key themes of this book, point the way forward. Rather than focusing on teacher-led models or confining pupils' thinking to local perspectives or capitalist themes, democratic and communitarian principles will seriously widen the agenda. Pupils will become active and innovative within a range of contexts, and become aware of their

Citizenship and Enterprise Education: Narrow versus Broad Perspectives		
	Narrow Focus	*Broad Focus*
Citizenship	Teaching about democracy The 'good' citizen Local/national perspectives Civic criticism	Enacting the principles of democracy The 'active' citizen Local, national and global perspectives Civic activism
Enterprise	Education for work Business entrepreneurship Individualism versus collectivism Isolated, prescribed projects	Innovation in a range of contexts Social entrepreneurship Individualism and collectivism

rights and corresponding obligations within their local, national and global community. They will be able to combine individual ambition with a drive towards social justice, and become exposed to a consultative, participative ethos outside the confines of individual projects.

The book examines how educational agendas once seen to be in conflict may instead be harmonised. It demonstrates that teachers cannot do justice to one agenda without drawing upon the other. A key theme is the examination of how bringing together citizenship and enterprise may help to redefine both educational agendas and ultimately enhance pupils' learning. Theoretical academic discussion is mixed with research evidence emerging from a Scottish-based study.

In Part I, the background to both educational agendas is explored and new theoretical perspectives presented. Chapter 1 examines the recent social, cultural and political developments that have given rise to the widening of the enterprise agenda and the renewed interest in citizenship education. This includes an examination of the perceived moral panic about eroding values among young people, alongside the wider recognition of the need to promote rights, democracy, sustainability and tolerance in schools. The chapter also explores the pressure teachers are currently under to combine this focus on ethics and values with the additional pressure of achieving educational excellence in terms of meeting the demands of externally-imposed goals, targets and league table results. The need to draw upon individualistic approaches to education as an agent for enhancing moral education is examined. The chapter raises some important issues, such as whether schools can be democratic institutions and whether existing enterprise practice can enable pupils to develop social, moral and ethical values.

The focus on individualism and collectivism is taken further in chapter 2. The origins of education for work, vocationalism, active learning and enterprise are examined. The chapter explores the emergence of neo-liberal enterprise, and the international evidence that suggests that this model is still a dominant force around the world. The chapter uses this evidence to examine recent British interest in the need for caring capitalism, and the way that this is currently influencing educational policy in Scotland. The influence of third way politics is examined with reference to the New Labour drive towards communitarianism and the emergence of education for citizenship. The chapter pinpoints the need for democratic approaches to teaching and learning and the vehicles for promoting this ethos, such as pupil councils, are examined. But the hierarchical, authoritarian approaches to school organisation that persist, and the impact on pupil motivation and learning, has to be explored. The chapter ends by examining British perspectives on education for citizenship and democracy, and pinpoints the broader focus evident in current policy.

The rhetoric associated with current policy agendas in Scotland is put to the test in Part II of the book, where we move towards examining current illustrations of practice in Scottish schools. This begins in chapter 3, where evidence from a small sample of Scottish primary schools is used to examine how teachers conceptualise the word enterprise and describe their vision for an enterprising teacher, pupil and school. Interview data is reported which illustrates evidence of classroom and whole-school practice. The chapter draws upon this evidence to examine the way in which enterprise and citizenship education may dovetail to produce innovative and successful results, as well as examining the perceived obstacles in terms of curriculum pressures and bureaucratic school structures.

The Scottish study is taken further in chapter 4 by exploring pupils' views. The chapter examines how pupils in the late stages of primary school and early stages of secondary school understand the meaning of the word 'enterprise'. Pupils' perceptions about entrepreneurs and the way in which particular job occupations may be carried out in an enterprising way are examined through evidence gathered from pupil discussions, questionnaires and cartoon-style drawings. The chapter examines how pupil responses span both ends of the communitarian spectrum and where their ideas about individualism and collectivist values meet.

Chapter 5 examines the need for schools to create a democratic framework for learning which enables pupils to participate actively in considering both social and community issues and to engage in enterprise education. The chapter focuses on the work of pupil councils and questions their potential for challenging aspects of school authoritarianism. Case study evidence from Scottish schools is presented, which focuses upon the work of the pupil councils in primary and secondary schools. The chapter draws upon this case study evidence as a means of examining the way in which individualism and collectivist values can connect within a democratic framework, as well as highlighting some of the obstacles.

One of the crucial arguments put forward in this book is the need for democratic principles to permeate all aspects of school life as a vehicle for citizenship and enterprise to flourish. Chapter 6 draws upon this principle to examine case studies of school practice in Scottish primary schools. These focus on pupil-led, community-based projects and the practice of discussing controversial issues in the classroom that are of particular interest to children. The way in which aspects of citizenship and enterprise education intertwine within these initiatives is of particular relevance.

Finally, chapter 7 looks back across the evidence arising from the case study schools and pinpoints the successes as well as the challenges. The theoretical debates are re-examined in terms of the research evidence and the chapter highlights some of the key questions that need further exploration in the light of current and future social, political and educational developments.

This book takes readers on a journey. It guides them through a macro-analysis of historical debates and the influences on enterprise and citizenship education. The theoretical principles that emerge from this discussion are used as the basis for an analysis of teacher and pupil attitudes, perceptions and school practice. This analysis leads readers back to a broader view of citizenship and enterprise. Each chapter ends with an opportunity to pause and reflect, suggesting activities that can be used as the basis for staff development and research. The book will interest academics as well as teachers, student teachers and those responsible for curriculum policy in citizenship and enterprise education. It offers new insights into how schools are responding to these agendas, and it will stimulate further debate about how policy and practice need to move forward.

PART I

THE CITIZENSHIP AND ENTERPRISE AGENDA

1

Professional dilemmas and chaos: moving forward with dual educational agendas

I n this new millennium, the world is arguably becoming increasingly democratic. The collapse of communist and military regimes around the world has been combined with an international focus on the need for human rights discourse. Yet the same democratic principles have been threatened by continual international fears about terrorism after 9/11. Fears and concerns about weakening community networks and the apparent rise of anti-social behaviour and increasing political apathy have made people aware of the need for intercultural tolerance and shared values throughout the developed world. But there is also increased international pressure to secure economic prosperity. Set within the context of globalisation, countries across the world are continually faced with pressures associated with economic improvement and international competitiveness.

Thus the 21st century requires young people to possess broad-ranging knowledge, multi-faceted skills and a wealth of personal dispositions. In many societies throughout the world, conventional wisdom says that schools need to take a leading role in equipping young people to function successfully in the wider world. Schools are being seen as agents of change and education as about preparing young people for a better world where human rights are promoted and young people are fully prepared for an active life within cosmopolitan communities across the world. At the same time education is still seen as a means of ensuring that young people are more employable and able to contribute towards the creation of competitive global economies.

These issues are as important in Britain as elsewhere. Debates about the role of enterprise education and education for citizenship are prominent but what is less understood is the possibility that both educational agendas can be infinitely more powerful when they are co-joined in educational policy and practice. This opening chapter explores some of the crucial developments taking place in school education. It examines the social and political influences that have created a dual focus on ethics and morality and economic dynamism in schools, leading to the widening of the enterprise agenda and a renewed interest in citizenship education. Important issues arise, such as whether democracy can be developed in authoritarian school structures and whether existing enterprise practice can enable pupils to develop social, moral and ethical values.

Increasing the focus on ethics, morality and economic dynamism

Many people today see the need for a stronger focus on ethics and morality in education. Totterdell (2000) pinpoints three closely related factors underpinning this. The first is the perceived moral breakdown in society, and the apparent erosion of values among young people. Lasch (1995: 80) refers to the view that many young people seem to be morally at sea and are failing to grasp the idea that values imply a form of moral obligation. He explores the commonly-held view that many young people 'insist they owe nothing to 'society' – an abstraction that dominates their attempts to think about social and moral issues'. The second factor is the perceived decay of our social fabric. Totterdell describes the times in which we live as an ephemeral, self-obsessed culture:

> The change-rich factor seems to increase exponentially and our demographics become ever more liquid. The result is the culture of the transitory, the momentary; a lust for immediate gratification, a universal concern with self. (Totterdell, 2000: 130)

4

The third is the erosion of professionalism and the move among public services, including teaching, towards a contract culture where neo-capitalist management strategies focus on efficiency and cost-effectiveness and where performance is judged against the outcomes of externally imposed targets. It seems that curative educational strategies that seek to raise pupil standards through improving teaching standards and practices have lessened the focus on morality and ethics in education, which in turn has demoralised some teachers. The renewed focus on values and ethics in education that reflect the principles underpinning democracy and social justice has perhaps been a response to the realisation that teaching should be a moral rather than a neutral endeavour.

Contemporary areas of intense interest and debate are increasing this drive towards ensuring that ethics is high on the educational agenda. For example, the increased focus on human rights discourse fostered a more pragmatic approach towards tackling racism in society. The report of the Stephen Lawrence Inquiry in 1999, which found the Metropolitian Police to be guilty of institutional racism, opened up a whole new debate about the extent of prejudice against ethnic minorities and the way in which inequalities of power are woven into the fabric of society (Faulks, 2000). The 2002 Nationality, Immigration and Asylum Act, which provided the legal basis for the dispersal of asylum seekers, has further increased the urgency for schools to recognise cultural diversity and facilitate equality of opportunity and social tolerance through multi-agency working (Barclay *et al*, 2003).

The increasing threat of terrorism following 9/11 has acted as a trigger for the global reassessment of what democracy actually means in terms of economic and cultural imperatives. 9/11 has been described as an attack on the fundamental principles of freedom, democracy and the rule of law and justice (Held, 2001; Osler, 2005: 5). The issues that have emerged from this crisis and the persistent threat of terrorism that has followed it have prompted fundamental questions about an individual's responsibility to support the democratic values of the country of which he or she is a citizen (Potter, 2002). It has also inspired educators to examine what schools are all about, what the mission of education in a democracy should be and how citizenship programmes can help schools to realise that mission (Graves, 2005).

The digital revolution seems to have made young people more aware of, and engaged in, single-issue politics. Many children are intensely interested in issues connected with environmental sustainability and coherent educational programmes have been argued for in the wake of debates about global warming, BSE, foot and mouth disease and genetically modified crops (Potter, 2002). *Agenda 21* is a comprehensive plan of action by organisations of the United Nations which was adopted by over 178 governments at the United Nations Conference on Environment and Development (UNCED) held in Rio de Janerio in 1992 (United Nations Sustainable Development, 1992). As a result issues related to aspects of sustainability have attracted intense global attention and 2005-2014 has been declared the United Nations Decade for Education for Sustainable Development. Many primary schools in Britain have responded to this by establishing eco-schools committees and a focus on development education programmes (see Shallcross *et al*, 2006). But media images in a global age also expose children to many more controversial social, political and humanitarian issues than ever before, such as the controversy that surrounded the Iraq War of 2003. Evidence has illustrated that pupils are keen to discuss such issues and that a programme on citizenship education needs to respond to this (see Maitles and Deuchar, 2004; 2004a; chapter 6 of this book).

Alongside all this is the continuing need for economic growth and prosperity. The Scottish Executive (2001) continues to encourage schools to focus upon employability skills, enabling young people to take their part in a prosperous, competitive economy. However, controversial new proposals to examine the possibility of prosecuting company directors for corporate culpable homicides has also increased the focus on a need for ethical forms of business (Deuchar, 2005). Thus, policy documentation needs to encourage not only a major expansion of the involvement of businesses in schools and the fostering of prosperity and wealth creation (Scottish Executive, 2002), but also to encourage the development of thoughtful, responsible and caring citizens (LTScotland, 2002).

This provides a glimpse of the huge challenges currently facing teachers. The perceived breakdown of social principles and values among young people has led to a renewed focus on ethics and moral education in schools. This has been bolstered by the recognition of racism, the need for acknowledging and respecting multiple cultural identities, concern over environmental sustainability issues and the humanitarian destruction caused by contemporary global conflict and terrorism. Citizenship education has come to be recognised as a vehicle for exploring many of these issues.

Alongside this, national concern over academic standards has led to externally imposed goals in the shape of league tables and exam results. The concern over the apparent productivity gap between Britain and other parts of Europe has reinforced the drive towards creating economic growth and prosperity through enterprise education but the need for compassion and business ethics is also high on the agenda. Teachers are caught in a dilemma: how can they seek excellence in terms of league table results and fostering economic drive and ambition while maintaining the ethical model they seek and are currently encouraged to promote in schools?

Mixing excellence with ethics

In a world strewn with competing agendas and conflicting priorities, it is difficult to imagine how teachers manage to harmonise their professional goals and principles with the current priorities of society and the many stakeholders who have a say in the educational process. Oliver and Heater (1994: 157) claim that school should be regarded as a 'micro-social or political community' and this makes the teacher's task of harmonising ethical and professional priorities even more essential.

How can teachers do their best work in preparing pupils for the wide set of roles that they will be expected to engage in when they are older? Gardner *et al* (2001) define people who do good work in terms of both excellence and ethics:

> People who do good work, in our sense of the term, are clearly skilled in one or more professional realms. At the same time, rather than merely following money or fame alone, or choosing the path of least resistance when in conflict, they are thoughtful about their

7

responsibilities and implications of their work. At best, they are concerned to act in a responsible fashion with respect towards their personal goals; their family, friends, peers and colleagues; their mission or sense of calling; the institutions with which they are affiliated; and, lastly, the wider world – people they do not know, those who will come afterwards, and, in the grandest sense, to the planet or to God. (Gardner *et al*, 2001: 3)

Many young professionals, including teachers, may find themselves in chaos: they strive to be loyal to the mission of the profession to which they were drawn, to maintain the standards appropriate to that profession and also to safeguard their own values, attitudes and moral principles but they are faced with market led, economy driven agendas. Being thoughtful, responsible and ethically driven in work situations is commendable, but the modern workplace is hugely complex. Expectations of external stakeholders often clash with the ethical standards inherent in a professional domain, and people ignore these expectations at their peril as 'today no professional realm can operate indefinitely if it clashes with the requirements of such stakeholders'. (Gardner *et al*, 2001: 26)

When cultural values clash with those of a particular professional domain, or when the expectations of stakeholders are in opposition to those of the profession, two types of dysfunctional consequences may arise:

When harmony in the social matrix falters, several consequences ensue … *anomie*, which occurs when norms break down to the extent that nobody any longer knows the right thing to do; and *alienation*, when norms become rigid and oppressive and nobody wants to do what has to be done. (Gardner *et al*, 2001: 30)

Reflecting upon the conditions that affect teachers in these ways is useful. Although teachers tend to have strong professional and ethical goals, guided by thoughtful and responsible personal drivers that may have attracted them to the profession in the first place, the nature of their work has become increasingly challenging. They are faced with new expectations, where education is seen as a consumer commodity and schools are run on a market model, operating along the same lines as commercial enterprises. Pupils and their parents have become the customers and consumers and politicians and school inspectors measure school outputs based on league tables and target-setting in relation to national priorities.

Much of this consumer-driven, competitive culture clashes with teachers' perceived educational mission, with its ethical and moral standards of equipping pupils with essential knowledge and life skills. Gardner *et al*'s perception of the forms of dysfunction that threaten many professions apply to education: while some teachers may be confused and unsure about the right path to take in their provision of education, others may have become oppressed by external influences. Many may feel frustrated in their attempts to harmonise these expectations with the more traditional ones that brought them into the profession.

Tensions between enterprise and citizenship education

Educationalists are faced with a huge challenge because education for citizenship is growing just when the enterprise education agenda is becoming stronger. In many teachers' minds the values underpinning these two aims appear contradictory; while enterprise has often been associated with fostering individual ambition, preparation for work and wealth creation, citizenship has more often been associated with the need for social and moral responsibility and for preparing young people with the knowledge required to play a role in the community. Nevertheless it is now recognised that young people can be enterprising within a whole range of contexts, as opposed to simply being encouraged to become business entrepreneurs.

In Britain, it is Margaret Thatcher who is most often associated with the promotion of enterprise in its narrowest sense; her assertion that there was 'no such thing as society, only individuals and families' (quoted in Davies *et al*, 2001: 264) was in the context of a growing interest in the free market, economic competitiveness and personal ambition. But as far back as 1984, views were emerging as to how enterprise should be interpreted more widely in schools:

> My own view is that we should be concerned with 'education to be enterprising' in the broadest sense, so that we can then allow ourselves the luxury of developing such specific aspects of it as 'education for self-employment' or 'education for enterprising

and creative use of leisure' or 'education for survival'. (Ball, 1984: 32)

Ball (1984) uses the example of the wide range of enterprising qualities shown by young people in developing countries which enable them to cope with adversity and grow in self-confidence and originality of thought. He uses examples of practice from the USA, Sweden and France to pinpoint the central roles of active learning, collective decision making and the relaxed relationship between teachers and pupils as the building blocks for creating enterprising schools. Yet even in 2004 we find Australian teachers still being accused of not understanding the needs of business and industry and pressure for schools to become driven by a consumerist approach (Billett, 2004). In Scotland, the Scottish Executive (2001) encourages schools to focus upon employability skills and enable young people to take their part in a prosperous, competitive economy. But while entrepreneurship is still associated with the setting up and running of a successful business in some minds, it is also seen as a form of caring capitalism, permitting opportunities for social endeavour (Scottish Executive, 2001; Hunter, 2003). Thus it is no surprise that the question on many teachers' minds is: what exactly is enterprise?

Self-confessed venture philanthropists have emerged such as Tom Hunter in Scotland, Anita Roddick in England and Bill Gates in the USA. This has led to more discussion about how young people can contribute towards economic strength while also helping the needy through charitable causes. Hunter's much publicised venture in 2005 to try to mitigate world poverty by donating millions to the African cause in conjunction with Bill Clinton is just one example of a new association between business entrepreneurship and global civic engagement.

However, the way in which existing enterprising approaches can lend themselves to the development of education for citizenship remains an enigma to schools of the 21st century. Davies *et al* (2001) sum up the apparently opposing dichotomies:

Teachers and schools are expected to play an essential transformative role in developing pupils' attitudes towards being competitive and enterprising and towards developing civic values ... can one, at the same time, be wholly competitive and wholly civic-minded? (Davies *et al*, 2001: 261)

In the early part of the 21st century, schools are facing the challenge of ensuring that both enterprise and citizenship are accommodated within the same curriculum. But the question posed by Davies *et al* (2001) illustrates the tensions that arise from this.

Mixing self-interest and moral education

While some teachers have a strong sense of the need for moral education and despair over the apparent collapse of the duty ethic in modern society, Goggin (2003: 68) questions their right to assume that 'duty is the only starting-point for morality'. He argues that morality would have no purpose if it did not connect at some point with human interests and that individual decisions about lifestyle and human well-being can lead to the development of a range of values, such as fairness, thoughtfulness and consideration of others. In short, self-interest can be a catalyst for developing a broad set of principles and values (Goggin, 2003).

In a Canadian study on the use of rights education in schools, Covell and Howe (2001: 31) found that there may be 'a contagion effect in which learning about one's own rights results in support for the rights of others'. Following the development of a children's rights curriculum in grade 8 classes in five different schools, it was found that adolescents showed higher self-esteem, higher levels of per-ceived peer and teacher support and indicated more support for the rights of others. The study concluded that rights education may be an effective agent of moral education (Covell and Howe, 2001).

Research also suggests that it may be essential for such education to involve democratic styles of teaching whereby pupils are en-couraged to have a say in matters concerning them, thus reflecting the principles underpinning the UN Convention on the Rights of the Child. Covell and Howe (2001) justify this clearly:

Teachers who are concerned with the maintenance of their authority in the classroom may be uncomfortable with allowing for the participation rights required by the curriculum and the Conven-tion. (Covell and Howe, 2001: 38)

So the re-emergence of values in education and a focus on moral education may, at first glance, be in direct conflict with individualism and the development of self-interest and freedom. However, recent research suggests that concentrating pupils' ideas on self may be a useful starting point for developing their awareness of the needs of others. Focusing on developing pupils' awareness of their own human rights can be a catalyst for enhancing their interest in wider values. This will achieve a move away from socialisation into school hierarchical structures towards greater emphasis on the child as an individual social actor. The way one secondary school pupil described a vision for an ideal school reinforces this idea:

> In my ideal school the whole philosophy that dominates schools now will be dropped ... we will no longer be treated like herds of an identical animal wanting to be civilised before we are let loose on the world. It will be recognised that it is our world too ... There will be no ridiculous hierarchy who don't even know us, to whom we are constantly proving ourselves. (Burke and Grosvenor, 2003: 94)

The co-joining of rights education and individualistic principles with collectivist views of society may be a useful way of enhancing the values and attitudes needed for 21st century society. Such an approach might reflect the way many young pupils think and feel in any case, mixing compassion with ambition and determination. However, research also suggests that this thinking and feeling approach should be accompanied by doing (Richardson, 1996; Osler and Starkey, 2002). Teachers should allow pupils to participate widely in decision making and to break down traditional school hierarchies which may act as a barrier to democratic education. The quotation above reflects the desperate need for ownership that many children might feel: ownership over their education, their future and the decisions involved in creating that future.

Pupil consultation and participation

Although a participative approach to school organisation is now recognised as a priority, the structures and pattern of relationships in schools have probably changed less than they should have (Baginsky and Hannam, 1999; Burke and Grosvenor, 2003). Articles 12 to 15 of the UN Convention on The Rights of the Child affirm children's right to freedom of expression and the freedom to form associations. The use of pupil councils has been recommended as a vehicle for the expression of active citizenship and democratic participation in schools. But some suggest that the experience of school councils is not yet particularly successful, and that far too many are tokenistic (Hannam, 1998; Dobie, 1998; Rowe, 2000)

Pupil consultation rests on the principle that pupils can bring something worthwhile to discussions about schooling and should be invited to talk about their experiences as learners, whereas pupil participation suggests membership of a community in which pupils are valued and respected contributors (Flutter and Ruddock, 2004). However, as Ruddock and Flutter (2004: 131) argue, there may be tension in some schools between teaching about government and democracy and enacting the principles of a democratic community. In such cases, pupil consultation and participation in matters related to learning and teaching need to be extended into every school classroom. This involves ensuring that pupils have a genuine say and are encouraged to engage in discussion about matters of particular interest to them, even down to negotiating what they are taught and how they learn (Deuchar, 2005a).

By its very nature the purpose of democracy is to provide a government by consent and should be informed by a range of values, such as freedom and equality (Carr, 2003). Indeed, a society may only be considered a just society if it is prepared to provide equal respect and fair treatment to all of its members. If a school is to be a democratic institution, teachers must have an understanding of the real principles underpinning democracy. White (1999: 61) argues that educating pupils to be true democrats involves the embodiment of values such as justice, freedom and personal autonomy into school practices. She argues that it involves instilling democratic dispositions or virtues among pupils so that they work within these practices 'in the right spirit' – that children need to become disposed to acquire the right knowledge and skills to pursue civic concerns. White highlights trust, in both personal and social terms, as a vital democratic virtue that schools should encourage among pupils. Pupils should be encouraged to develop trustworthy personal relationships and also to have trust in the school's system of rules, procedures and methods.

These views lead us to consider whether schools reflect these democratic practices and, where they do, whether pupils are equipped with the dispositions needed to embrace them wholeheartedly. Perhaps a starting-place is to ensure that pupils are aware of their own rights of participation as a means of enabling them to engage in the scrutiny of democratic principles and practices. Schools may encourage this type of participative, consultative ethos through creating democratic classrooms where pupils have a say in matters relating to learning and teaching (Maitles and Gilchrist, 2003) or through encouraging the discussion of controversial issues of particular interest to them (Maitles and Deuchar, 2004; 2004a).

This consultative, participative approach in the classroom may have a direct impact on pupils' engagement and, as a result, their learning and behaviour. Indeed, Ruddock and Flutter (2004: 133) argue that if pupils feel they matter and are respected in schools, they are 'more likely to commit themselves to the school's purposes'. In addition, if teaching and the conditions of learning are experienced as congenial, pupils are 'more likely to commit themselves to learning and develop positive identities as learners'. Harber (2004) has discussed the implications of the continued presence of authoritarian structures in schools and made links between this form of socialisation and the expression of violent behaviour among pupils.

In spite of this, evidence from around the globe, including Africa, Asia, North America and many parts of Europe, suggests that schools have retained a strong ethos of authoritarianism in both their organisation and teaching methods (Harber, 2004). Chapter 2 develops these debates, while later chapters consider the vehicles for promoting a participative, consultative ethos which might enable aspects of enterprise and citizenship education to be harmonised.

Summary

Several areas of development provide the backdrop to the chapters that follow:

- ▨ A broadening perception of the meaning of the word enterprise beyond its original association with individualism and the thrusting entrepreneur model associated with business, making it difficult for schools to define what to associate with enterprising behaviour.

- ▨ A renewed focus on ethics, morality and citizenship education, stemming from the perceived worry about youth alienation and leading to the expectation that schools should promote civic-minded values through their practice in citizenship and enterprise education.

- ▨ The sensitive issue for schools of whether democracy can be developed in authoritarian structures and whether existing practice in citizenship and enterprise education can enable pupils to experience an authentic model of democratic decision-making (Harber, 2004; Maitles and Deuchar, 2004; 2004a).

In the next chapter, the origins and development of enterprise and citizenship education are examined. It considers the extent to which current perspectives on enterprise education may enable the development of active, ethical citizenship in schools.

Pause for reflection

Before reading further about the current perspectives that underpin citizenship and enterprise, it might be useful to explore your own initial thoughts about the two agendas. Jot down some answers to the questions below: an instinctive reaction is best at this stage, as you may want to reconsider these after reading the next few chapters.

- ▨ How would you define the word enterprise?
- ▨ What would you expect to see in an enterprising school?
- ▨ What qualities would you associate with an enterprising pupil?
- ▨ What qualities would you associate with an enterprising teacher?
- ▨ How would you define a responsible citizen?
- ▨ What qualities would you expect to see in an active citizen?
- ▨ How would you define a democratic school?

2

A third way for education:
the challenges of reconciling citizenship and enterprise

Recent developments have raised questions about the real purpose of education and the fundamental role of teachers in society. It could be said that schools have succumbed to the pressure to conform to market forces while still trying to represent themselves as crucibles of morality, justice and values (Burke and Grosvenor, 2003). Two key educational agendas have been at the centre of much of the debate in recent years: enterprise education and education for citizenship. In this chapter the background to these two agendas is examined, along with the way they have evolved in response to changing social, cultural and political thinking.

Vocationalism and active learning in schools

The promotion of enterprise education, preparation for work and lifelong learning has recently received multi-million pound funding of initiatives, the national recruitment of enterprise advisers and a national enterprise agenda throughout Britain. Hayward (2004) acknowledges that such developments are typically traced to the Ruskin College Speech given by Prime Minister Jim Callaghan in 1976 but argues that the idea of vocationalism is much older and stems from at least the time of the Samuelson Commission on Technical Instruction of 1882-84 (Ryan, 2003; Hayward, 2004).

A key figure in the development of a vocational perspective in education was John Dewey. Through his laboratory school Dewey (1938) tried to persuade education to develop in line with the pace of change within industry and to encourage schools to promote pupil individuality and autonomy and experiential, contextualised learning. Dewey's vision for education encompassed a model of industry in which people have an active and creative part to play that should be mirrored in schools (Jamieson *et al*, 1988). He condemned the institutional school model of the 19th century with its apparent isolation from the realities of life experience:

> From the standpoint of the child, the great waste in the school comes from his inability to utilise the experience he gets from outside the school in any complete and free way within the school itself; while, on the other hand, he is unable to apply to daily life what he is learning at school. That is the isolation of the school – its isolation from life. (Dewey, 1915: 67)

From the late 19th century onwards sections of British industry made attempts to promote vocational schooling, although the growing prosperity following the second world war reduced social unrest and produced changes in the demand for labour, and this resulted in a temporary decrease in vocationalism (Shilling, 1989). The Brunton Report in Scotland (1963) aimed to ensure that young people were once again motivated by the vocational impulse (SED, 1963: 24) and more prepared for opportunities in further education. Brunton's vision was combined with the need for creating a cadre of teachers who would ensure that vocational approaches would be used to increase pupils' intrinsic motivation across the curriculum (SED, 1963; Weir, 1988). This vision was later put into a wider context by the Scottish Education Department's Consultative Committee on the Curriculum (SCCC), which saw vocational schooling as being co-equal with social and moral education (Weir, 1988). However, much of Brunton's vision was misinterpreted as being a remedy only for non-academic pupils in secondary schools, while the more academic continued to be educated via didactic approaches.

Improved living standards and low unemployment in the 1960s were followed by a period of technological and social change. A decline in the manufacturing industry was accompanied by the collapse of the apprenticeship system and economic recession in the 1970s which led to increased levels of youth unemployment, poor working conditions and low wages (Shilling, 1989). Many industrialists took the view that schools were not equipping students with the knowledge, skills and attitudes necessary to stimulate economic growth. Thus, a renewed focus on education for work and vocationalism emerged:

> From a dominant focus on universities and the career destinations of highly qualified students, industrial interest widened to a concern that schools should promote the skills, attitudes and knowledge required in different echelons of the economy. (Shilling, 1989: 44)

The pressure on schools to promote education that was relevant to the needs of industry added to the demand for more active forms of learning. This style of learning, with its emphasis on pupil discovery, autonomy, responsibility and co-operation, was regarded as a means of improving student motivation and encouraging deeper learning. Essentially, the active learning approach was seen as intrinsically more enjoyable than passive forms of learning and a useful vehicle for preparing pupils for the world of work and industry (Jamieson *et al*, 1988).

The positioning of education-industry relations as a central part of the political agenda was strengthened by the Great Debate launched in 1976 by Jim Callaghan. His Ruskin College speech focused on the need for schools to equip young people with the skills, attitudes and knowledge required by industry. The subsequent launch in 1977 of the Education for an Industrial Society Project (EISP) in Scotland was paralleled by the Schools Council Industry Project (SCIP) in England and Wales. The key focus of the EISP project was to review and enhance the methods used by secondary schools to prepare pupils for work in an industrial society. But over-reliance on volunteers and some short-term secondments weakened the project's coherence and the Munn/Dunning Development Programme on certification undermined teachers' commitment towards the initiative (Weir, 1988; Lynch, 1992; Gregory, 1999). Nevertheless, the debate about education as a valuable means of equipping pupils for the world of work was set to continue.

Education for work and enterprise

After the General Election in 1979, Margaret Thatcher expressed the desire to develop more enterprising individuals through the education system and emphasised the need for children to leave school with a sound understanding of what industry and commerce had to offer (Watts, 1984). Thatcher's focus was on neo-liberalism, personal gain and the need for economic revival through the ending of the anti-enterprise culture that had existed since 1945 (DuGay, 1991; Faulks, 1998; Shacklock *et al*, 2000). The creation of the TVEI in 1983 signalled the beginning of a comprehensive British programme for equipping young people for the demands of working life (Jamieson *et al*, 1988; Shuttleworth, 1993). The school curriculum was related to the world of work, to enable pupils to gain experience of work placements and to develop generic skills in pupils, such as communication, problem solving and teamwork (Shuttleworth, 1993).

Jamieson *et al* (1988: 75) trace the initial market leader of the idea of enterprise education to Young Enterprise, founded back in 1963, with the aim of providing young people aged 15 to 19 with an 'elementary working knowledge of the organisation, methods and practice of commerce and industry through first-hand experience'. However, the development of the enterprise culture in British schools since then has generally been characterised by 'shadowy ideas' (Ritchie, 1991: 315), which encompass a broad range of educational initiatives (MacDonald, 1991; Shacklock *et al*, 2000). Enterprise education appeals to all shades of the political spectrum:

> Education for 'self-employment', 'enterprise', 'competitiveness' and 'mini-companies' has – for some observers – an unmistakable bluish hue. While curriculum material concerning 'communes', 'cooperatives', 'mini-co-operatives', 'right-to-work action', 'assertiveness' ... seem to others to be decidedly pink. (Law, 1983: 2)

The focus on individuality and personal gain fits well with conservative politics, while the focus on cooperative learning might satisfy those on the left. But which value is most dominant in the enterprise education agenda?

20

Development of an enterprise culture in schools across the world

The expansion of the enterprise agenda in Britain since the 1980s has been paralleled in many other parts of the world. In some cases expansion has been strongly associated with a concern about growing youth unemployment, skills shortages and the need for economic improvement and the focus has been on individualism. Smyth (1999: 435) describes the recent emergence of enterprise education in Australia in an attempt to 'relocate the problem of the youth labour market in schools'. The enterprise agenda is thus being seen as a solution to economic problems by enabling students to acquire skills in innovation, networking and enterprising behaviour. It has been argued that the Australian federal government initiative *Enterprise Education in Schools Programme* hinges on the importance of people working for themselves and gaining experience of how small businesses operate (Smyth, 1999: 439).

Smyth (1999) refers to the OECD/CERI (1989) distinction between narrow definitions of enterprise education focusing mainly on business entrepreneurship and broad definitions that focus more on creating competences that enable flexibility, creativity and adaptability. He believes that such distinctions are located within the same crucible and that features of adaptability, flexibility, and teamwork are still ultimately serving the interests of business. In spite of the alternative rhetoric, he argues that enterprise education serves to narrow the Australian curriculum. It appears to direct pupil learning towards individualistic, business values and expunges the focus on compassion, justice, education for a better world and the need to challenge the *status quo* (Smyth, 1999).

Attempts to camouflage the underlying political and social motivations underpinning enterprise education are also an issue in South Africa. Matseleng Allais (2003) outlines the introduction of the National Qualifications Framework (NQF) as an apparent symbol of the development of a single, egalitarian education system for all as part of the post-apartheid transition to democracy in the early 1990s. But although the NQF appears to be driven by a focus on social justice and empowerment, this masks the underlying motivation to enable transition towards a 'neo-liberal economy' (Matseleng

Allais, 2003: 307). The outcomes based education system has been strongly associated with neo-liberal economic policies aimed at making the South African economy globally competitive. Thus the tensions between enabling the transition to democracy or to economic success seem irreconcilable and the neo-liberal agenda has come to dominate.

A wave of vocational education and training in Canada has been based upon a market-based model (Taylor, 2005: 330). Policy makers in Ontario have emphasised the need for voluntary partnerships with businesses coordinated by brokers, causing employers to define the work skills that schools should promote (Taylor, 2005). In China, work-study programmes aimed at ending the elitist nature of Chinese education have evolved into creating school enterprises. As described by Fouts and Chan (1997), technical specialists combine with teachers to run factories, farms, construction companies and service industries, based on market demand. Financial gains that are channelled towards supplementing education funds increase the incentives for teachers, while students are encouraged to participate in such labour education (Fouts and Chan, 1997). In Germany, by contrast, a dual system of on-the-job training and school-based vocational education relies on social partnerships between employers, schools, the unions and the government. This system seeks to ensure that learning is free of direct economic ends or purposes (Holt, 1987; Taylor, 2005).

Developments in these countries reveal tensions between educational rhetoric and practice. While some countries distinguish between broad and narrow approaches, the word 'enterprise' is often used as a substitute for 'business' (Peters, 1992; Smyth, 1999). Such an agenda is viewed as an antidote for the need for strengthening world economies and international success. Evidence suggests that policy and practice results in an over-emphasis on the promotion of self-interest which ultimately stifles the promotion of active and ethical citizenship. However, there are exceptions where enterprise education is fostered through genuine partnerships and the promotion of an agenda which is free from the economic stranglehold.

The nature of enterprise education in Britain

Enterprise in British primary schools has often taken the form of a business enterprise project where pupils work in teams to create, market and sell a product for financial profit and learn about the key concepts of a business. Alternatively, children may be involved in a community-based project, where they learn about community support structures and how they must anticipate and respond to changing needs, or an environmental project where they develop an aspect of the local environment such as creating and maintaining the school garden or playground, and learn that beneficial change is possible if some individual or group is prepared to take the initiative (Brownlow *et al*, 1998). The Enterprise and Industry Education Unit at Durham University Business School (DUBS) produced research indicating that children should emerge from enterprise projects more motivated, confident, creative, flexible, able to cope with failure, able to work in teams and able and willing to take risks (Ireland, 1993).

However the emphasis in Britain, as in so many other countries and due perhaps to the scapegoating of schools for the lack of economic success, has generally been led by the business enterprise model. Even in the early 1980s, Ball (1984) identified this as a cause for concern in the light of the enterprising qualities arising in young people in developing countries and in parts of Europe and the USA. He cites the holistic enterprising practice in the On Location schools in San Francisco that enabled pupils to focus on creativity across the curriculum. In Sweden evidence of pupil cooperatives was emerging at this time, while the French were creating enterprising schools which were focused on environmental issues and enabling disadvantaged groups to become active in their local community. Some writers (Kearney and Russell-Green, 1991; Shacklock *et al*, 2000: 54) have identified the enterprising teacher as one who focuses on enabling greater student autonomy, focuses teaching on relevant experiences, encourages teamwork and a focus on student review and self-assessment.

The Scottish Executive identifies the role of enterprise education networks in delivering the vision of productivity growth, competitiveness and prosperity (Scottish Executive, 2001). The White Paper

21st Century Skills: Realising our Potential (DfES, 2003) and the Scottish Executive's (2003) *Life through Learning; Learning through Life* signal continued commitment towards developing pupils' skills for increased productivity, innovation, profitability and employability *as well as* fairness and inclusivity (Hayward, 2004). At the same time, the Scottish Executive's *Determined to Succeed* underlines the continued commitment towards enterprise in education as a means to creating dynamic, enterprising individuals who can both improve the quality of their own lives and contribute towards economic strength:

> The Review Group's vision is of a more successful and prosperous Scotland where young people are determined to succeed and where innovation, wealth creation and entrepreneurship are valued ... Young people in Scotland must have the best possible experiences of Enterprise in Education so they can contribute to an enterprising, successful Scotland as employees, employers and entrepreneurs. (Scottish Executive, 2002: 1)

The Scottish Executive also stresses the need for expressing enterprising qualities within a range of roles and to use this as the basis for contributing to both economic development and social renewal:

> Encouraging enterprising values – a 'can do, will do' attitude – in our schoolchildren is not just about producing the business people and entrepreneurs of tomorrow. It is the route to a more enterprising Scotland, where all our people understand the contribution they can make as citizens, both to society and the economy. And where individuals have the self-confidence and belief in their ability to succeed in whatever they choose. (Scottish Executive, 2003a)

British policy documentation has hence directed teachers' thinking away from education for work and enterprise to a model of enterprise education as a means of both economic and social entrepreneurship. However, the extent to which this actually enables the development of areas such as active, ethical citizenship is still in question.

The re-emergence of citizenship education and communitarianism

Although the term citizenship had been in use in the English education system from about 1880 to 1950, a lull in interest after the welfare state was established removed it from the education agenda for 40 years (Oliver and Heater, 1994). The first signs of revival came in 1988 following Douglas Hurd's discussion of the need for active citizenship as a form of moral re-alignment (Hyland, 1991; Potter, 2002). Active citizenship was a principal theme of the 1988 Conservative Party conference. Margaret Thatcher emphasised the need for personal, individual effort to enhance a sense of community (Schwarz, 1989). But citizenship education was still seen as a function of social control, and the active citizen was narrowly interpreted as someone who pays their taxes, obeys the law and takes care of their neighbour (Cunningham and Lavalette, 2004).

An attempt to introduce citizenship education in schools in 1988 as part of the cross-curricular themes underpinning the new national curriculum in England proved unsuccessful, due in part to the failure to create an overriding theme related to active civic engagement. The proposals became more pragmatic after 1997 under New Labour at a time of constitutional reform. This included the 1998 Human Rights Act, increased awareness of the 1990 UN Convention on the Rights of the Child, the establishment of a Scottish Parliament and a Welsh Assembly and the creation of an assembly and elected mayor for London (Osler and Starkey, 2001). The political evolution associated with New Labour's decision to drop clause 4 and to create a third way between capital and welfare has focused on strong underlying dualities (Giddens, 2000). These include the need to create a parallel focus on patriotism, globalisation and cosmopolitan pluralism, authority and democracy and rights and responsibilities and to create a link between economic restoration and cultural and moral regeneration (Giddens, 1998; Lawson, 2001; Deuchar, 2004). Giddens (1998: 65) argues that third way politics looks for 'a new relationship between the individual and the community', as Tony Blair has stated:

> The question for today is whether we can achieve a new relationship between the individual and society, in which the individual

25

> acknowledges that, in certain key respects, it is only by working to-
> gether in a community of people that the individual's interests can
> be advanced. (Blair, 1996, quoted in Faulks, 1998: 204).

The bringing together of seemingly incompatible principles has characterised New Labour's policies and vision. 'Not only this but also that' statements are common in Blair's rhetoric (Fairclough (2000: 10). Grafting inclusive and socially-oriented outcomes on to the ideology of the New Right, in an attempt to avoid both the statism of socialism and the market fundamentalism of neo-liberalism, has been a key aim of his party's politics (Faulks, 2000). Communitarianism seeks to create a route between old socialist ideals and recent neo-liberal individualism where community members have rights as individuals but also obligations to society (Lawson, 2001). Loxley and Thomas (2001) discuss the complex role for schools in delivering a model of citizenship education under-pinned by communitarian principles with the dual aims of en-couraging individualism as a means of economic restoration com-bined with collectivist approaches to cultural and moral regenera-tion.

Political and social apathy?
There are other reasons for the renewed interest in citizenship education. Low levels of voter turnout in national elections in the USA, France and Britain have caused concern, almost moral panic, about young people's apparent disengagement with the democratic processes of public life. The growing realisation that young people are more inclined to vote for the winner of national television pro-grammes such as *Big Brother* than they are to vote in local or national elections has added urgency to the development of a citizenship agenda grounded in civic engagement (Mills, 2002).

Yet, there is plenty of evidence that young people are more engaged with single-issue politics than ever before. In 2003 more than 600 protests against the Iraq war took place around the globe; anti-war gatherings in London, Glasgow and Belfast coincided with a world-wide weekend of protest with hundreds of rallies and marches in almost 60 countries which involved 30 million people (BBC News, 2003; Cunningham and Lavalette, 2004). In the USA protests in large cities such as New York, Chicago and Los Angeles coincided with rallies in smaller towns such as Gainesville, Georgia, Macomb, Illinois and Juneau, Alaska (CNN, 2003).

In July 2005 over 225,000 people took to the streets of Edinburgh to lead an international call on world leaders attending the G8 Summit to take action against poverty. The *Make Poverty History* campaign aimed to end poverty by helping to bring about trade justice, more and better aid and the full and final cancellation of third world debt. While children and adolescents around the globe wore the symbol of the campaign, a white wrist band, many were also heavily involved in fundraising campaigns and took part in the peace protests. Whatever people may have thought about *Live 8*, it undoubtedly had the capacity to mobilise large numbers of young people to make a response to a humanitarian cause (Deuchar, 2005b). Millions of young people became actively engaged in fundraising campaigns for Africa, and school pupils talked openly of the connection between this and the ongoing war against terrorism (Deuchar, 2005b). Thus, although young people's disillusionment in parliamentary politics may have grown, it seems that their interest in political issues and involvement in grassroots campaigns is alive and well.

Although young people are portrayed in the media as walking around in hooded tops brandishing knives, recent reports suggest that youth crime has fallen to the lowest levels for 25 years (Waiton, 2001; 2006). But the notion of disaffected youth has fed demands for an increased focus on moral values, culminating in the recent creation of Blair's respect agenda:

> Too many people still suffer from the anti-social behaviour of a minority and feel powerless to stop it. That is why the Respect drive is so important. To truly tackle disadvantage and build a dynamic, prosperous and socially just society, we must offer the support and challenge needed to tackle anti-social behaviour, and its causes, and ensure that we all pass on decent values and standards of behaviour to our children. (Blair, quoted in Respect Task Force, 2006)

The renewed interest in education for citizenship in Britain has coincided with an evolving political model and a growing sense of social unease. Constitutional reform has brought wider issues of national identity and community awareness to the fore yet young people are being branded as both apathetic and threatening, despite much evidence to the contrary (Waiton, 2001). The New Labour drive towards ethical rather than scientific socialism, which transcends the limits of neo-liberalism and the older Labourite ideologies, has generated communitarian ideals (Faulks, 1998; Loxley and Thomas, 2001). The associated need to create ambitious individuals who demonstrate social respect and tolerance is a challenge to education. Schools are expected to respond to a new multi-faceted education agenda.

What is education for citizenship?

We need to draw upon these debates in order to reach a clearer definition of what we should hope to see in schools today. Cogan and Derricott (2000) argue that the changing nature of the world requires a multi-dimensional approach that does not focus purely on the good citizen but encompasses a commitment to participation in public life. But since active citizenship is a contested term meaning anything from helping a neighbour to orchestrating a major social campaign (Lawson, 2001), where do teachers begin?

The debate concerning maximal versus minimal approaches to citizenship education is at the heart of the issue. In a minimal approach pupils learn about their own rights, personal identities and being decent, law-abiding citizens, whereas a maximal model encourages a sense of obligation to others and a willingness to undertake change on a local, national and global scale (Davies *et al*, 2001; Osler and Starkey, 2002). A maximal approach encourages pupils to become agents of social change, developing enquiring minds and the skills for participation (Oliver and Heater, 1994; Wilkins, 2001). This requires institutional support to involve pupils in making decisions in school within a framework of democratic consultation (Crick and Porter, 1978).

Channelling international perspectives on democracy into schools

There is a gap between the acknowledged need for such democratic participation in schools and the practical realisation of this goal (Forrester, 2003). Harber (1995) notes that in spite of the plethora of educational conferences on citizenship and democracy in Israel, the USA, Denmark, Norway, South Africa and Britain, international approaches to schooling are still authoritarian. In one Canadian study cited by Harber (1995) less than one fifth of pupils surveyed in Ontario felt that teachers were in the habit of asking for their opinions and ideas. In Britain Charles Handy has compared the organisational styles of secondary schools to those of a prison, where pupils have no place to call their own and are often forbidden to communicate with one another (Harber, 1995). In Africa, China and South America many teachers adopt a didactic approach and insist on unquestioned authority (Harber, 1995).

In Canada emphasis on rigour and standards in education, led by the introduction of provincial testing and a new Ontario curriculum, has left teachers feeling they are implementers of government-initiated policies rather than agents of change (Schweisfurth, 2006). Although civics education has become a compulsory part of the curriculum, with a focus on informed, purposeful and active citizenship, Schweisfurth (2006) found that the promotion of global citizenship education is rarely prioritised by Ontario schools or teachers and that many secondary school departments are described as ghettoised, preventing the potential for cross-disciplinary work to flourish (Schweisfurth, 2006).

On both sides of the Atlantic there have been pupil strikes against the Iraq war of 2003. Tens of thousands of American schoolchildren marched out of their classes calling for 'books not bombs' (Cunningham and Lavalette, 2004: 259). Pupils in Switzerland, Greece, Denmark, Sweden, Germany, Italy, Spain, Australia and Britain did the same (Phipps, 2003). The passion with which pupils engaged in the protests challenged those who claimed that children were too young to debate or react to such issues. One ten year-old in Liverpool said:

> Bush and Blair will kill thousands of Iraqi children, just like me and my friends. My teachers told me I was too young to protest, but if I'm too young to protest, they're too young to be killed. (Diane, aged 10, quoted in Cunningham and Lavalette, 2004: 259).

In spite of children's intense interest in these issues and their willingness to enact social change through peaceful protest, the dominant view of the educational establishments in North America, Portugal, France and elsewhere was that the strikes were an excuse for truancy. Many children faced disciplinary proceedings and suspensions (Harber, 2004).

There is a discrepancy between international thinking about education for citizenship and what is actually promoted in schools. Schools in the USA and many parts of Europe have not changed their practices. Hierarchical, bureaucratic forms of school organisation still dominate, teachers still favour a didactic approach to teaching and view pupil initiative and willingness to engage in social activism as deserving punishment.

International classroom responses

Evidence from around the globe indicates that the current models of education for citizenship tend to promote active participation only within the confines of existing social norms. Davies and Issitt (2005) report on evidence emerging from coursework in citizenship education in England, Canada and Australia. Their analysis of textbooks, the existence of which are themselves an indication of the non-radical approach taken towards teaching citizenship education, illustrate a strongly conservative model. The texts focus on national rather than global issues and thus limit the scope of citizenship education:

> On the one hand the justification for citizenship education development rests on the need for greater participation in order to strengthen democratic structures and processes further; on the other hand citizens are perceived as subjects to be moulded to state authority ... this latter tendency can be seen particularly in textbooks. The citizen is free and not free at the same time. (Davies and Issitt, 2005: 405)

Evidence from other parts of the world also reveals deficit models. A study in France showed evidence of restricted models of textbook-based programmes that failed to motivate pupils (Osler and Starkey, 2002). In the USA, civics education programmes do little to challenge the unilateralist version of patriotism advanced by the Bush administration since 9/11 (Boyte, 2003). In England, Ofsted has found evidence of a plethora of unsuccessful lessons that encourage pupils to talk about the dangers of underage sex and drug abuse but ignore issues which pupils want to discuss, such as third world debt, international terrorism and anti-war campaigns (Cunningham and Lavalette, 2004).

But there are isolated success stories. Forrester (2003) identifies global sites of innovative citizenship education in Albania, Bulgaria, Ireland and Italy which emphasise inclusiveness, pluralism and the need for local and global partnerships. In the USA Boyte (2003) notes team projects aimed at fighting discrimination and Islamophobia, such as when 10 and 11 year-old African Americans were trying to educate their school about Afghanistan. Schweisfurth (2006: 46) reveals how a group of Canadian social science teachers have been able to inject a focus on global citizenship into their work in spite of the constraints of a state curriculum and a strong focus on the attainment agenda. Pupils were encouraged to be radical in their confrontational approach to civic action by raising awareness of the dangers of landmines and distributing pamphlets about the environmental dangers of four-wheeled drive vehicles. While the teachers gained confidence in using these approaches through forming networks, it was clear that the culture in schools worked against their aspirations:

> While the teachers were not actively discouraged by their colleagues ... there was agreement that 'that kind of activism isn't really part of the image of teaching' and that 'the bureaucracy in teaching discourages it'. (Schweisfurth, 2006: 48).

It seems that isolated groups of teachers may be doing exceptional work in many countries in enabling pupils to learn about citizenship by engaging in global forms of civic action. However, these teachers struggle against bureaucracy, conservatism and prescribed curricula that seek to stifle their enthusiasm and the pupils' motivation.

National policies and guidelines in England and Scotland

In Britain the Advisory Group on Citizenship's report, *Education for Citizenship and the Teaching of Democracy in Schools* (QCA, 1998), led to the inclusion of citizenship in the national curriculum of England and Wales. The origins of the report lie in the release of the first New Labour White Paper on education in 1997, *Excellence in Schools* (Department of Education and Employment, 1997), which highlighted the need to strengthen the teaching of citizenship and politics in schools. Kerr (1999) describes the QCA's position on citizenship education as being about the development of pupils' knowledge, skills and values relevant to democratic practice and including awareness of individual rights and responsibilities, understanding of world affairs and a sense of the value of community improvement.

T.H. Marshall (1950) classically defined citizenship as encompassing civil, political and social elements, and the QCA define social and moral responsibility as including the need for pupils to learn self-confidence and responsible behaviour. Community involvement is learning about and becoming helpfully involved in the life and concerns of their communities and political literacy involves teaching children about how to make themselves effective in public life through conflict resolution and decision making in relation to local, regional, European and international affairs (QCA, 1998; Kerr, 1999).

In England the content of education for citizenship is defined in terms of a framework of specific learning outcomes for each key stage, as opposed to detailed programmes of study. This offers flexibility to schools, based on local conditions and opportunities. The Advisory Report specifically addresses the need for active citizenship, encouraging positive engagement between schools and their communities (QCA, 1998). However, as Davies *et al* (2005: 77) note, the report's multiple references to the nation state does not suggest a strong focus on an international/global perspective.

The apparently generic view of the purposes of the citizenship agenda is supported by LTScotland, (2002) in *Education for Citizenship in Scotland – a Paper for Discussion and Development*. LTScotland (2002: 5) views the 'knowledgeable citizen' as one who is aware of the 'complexity of the economic, ethical and social issues and dilemmas that confront people and thinks that young people should also possess personal qualities such as 'self-esteem, confidence, initiative, determination and emotional maturity' to develop generic skills. This includes an ability to work independently and in collaboration with others and to make informed decisions, persevering in the face of setbacks. Finally, modern citizens should possess values and dispositions that allow them to develop informed and reasoned opinions, express and critically evaluate other people's views and to value cultural and community diversity. LT-Scotland imply that pupils' capacity to think and act creatively and to be enterprising in their approach to solving a problem or resolving an issue may allow expression of citizenship capability.

Summary

This chapter has examined the background to the dual agenda of citizenship and enterprise education. The main issues are that:

- ▓ The dominance of third way politics has been highlighted as the driving force behind the need for educating today's pupils to be active in both strengthening economic success and renewing social values.

- ▓ The political rhetoric surrounding enterprise education has changed to a focus on social entrepreneurship. But much international evidence suggests that the neo-liberal agenda prevails and that a great deal of policy and practice is focused on an individualistic, business-related model.

- ▓ Education for citizenship has emerged as a means of growing social and political engagement through democratic participation in schools. But evidence from countries around the world indicates that schools remain hierarchical and authoritarian in nature and that approaches towards citizenship follow a narrow, conservative model. A more maximal approach, where pupils act as agents of change in relation to wider, global issues which genuinely interest them, is found only in isolated cases.

■ In Scotland recent guidelines provide a maximal approach to education for citizenship and enterprise, focusing on both individualistic and collectivist values and encouraging pupil consultation. Within this, enterprise is seen as an essential building block for enabling creativity and innovation.

Scottish teachers and pupils need to be clear about the meaning of enterprise and its relationship with active civic engagement. Schools should be creating democratic approaches to learning, based on pupil consultation and participation. Part II explores how these principles are becoming a reality in Scottish schools.

Pause for thought and reflection

How clear are you about what you associate with education for citizenship, with enterprise education and with global education? Do a brainstorming exercise, identifying as many aspects of school practice that you can think of that relate to citizenship. Then do the same exercise in relation to enterprise and again with global education. Teachers and student teachers can do this in groups with other colleagues as the basis of a staff development day or seminar. Each list of ideas could be presented on a poster as the basis for further discussion. If you find that many of the ideas overlap, this is a good sign: a maximal approach to citizenship and enterprise means that one agenda cannot be completely separated from the other. Including a global dimension is also desirable. Putting the three lists together could provide the basis for developing a policy on enterprising global citizenship.

PART II

TEACHERS', PUPILS' AND SCHOOLS' RESPONSES TO CITIZENSHIP AND ENTERPRISE EDUCATION

3

'It's about letting go of the reins': teachers' views on enterprising behaviour and enterprise education

The current rhetoric surrounding enterprise education in Britain focuses on aligning moral considerations with corporate individualism (Hyland, 1991; Potter, 2002). Policy developments tell us that schools should seek to enable students to engage actively in both economic and social renewal (QCA, 1998; LTScotland, 2002; Scottish Executive, 2002). This chapter reports on a sample of Scottish headteachers' and classroom teachers' views on the meaning of enterprise and enterprise education, gathered during 2002 to 2004. It explores the nature of school practice in sample schools and the way in which attitudes and values evolved over three school years. It shows how communitarianism as a theoretical model emerged as the major theme in these teachers' conceptualisations of enterprise, reflecting the wider political and social evolution in Britain.

The research context

Scottish primary schools (age range 5 to 11) that would provide a diverse range of school types and socio-economic contexts were chosen for study. Ten schools were selected in light of information from Her Majesty's Inspectorate of Education (HMIE), LTScotland, local and national publicity materials and the database of the Centre for Studies in Enterprise, Career Development and Work at the

University of Strathclyde. The schools were in seven local council areas from northeast to southwest Scotland but mainly in the central belt. Both denominational and non-denominational schools were selected, and there were several inner city schools plus rural and schools in small towns. One school had a high proportion of ethnic minority pupils but most were almost exclusively white. Some schools were in affluent social contexts but several were located in deprived areas and at least one was in a socially deprived area with a high level of drug-related crime.

The sample schools also had differing experiences of enterprise endeavour. Some schools had won awards for their enterprise practice, whereas others were less high profile and might be only starting out on their journey with enterprise. Within each sample school, one class was selected as a case study from primary 4 (P4) (aged 8), primary 5 (P5) (aged 9) or primary 6 (P6) (aged 10). Semi-structured interviews were conducted with each classroom teacher and headteacher in 2002. These interviews enabled me to identify teachers' perceptions of the type of behaviour they regarded as enterprising, the purpose and role of enterprise education and to judge the consistency with which national policy was being translated into practice in enterprise and citizenship education in these schools. Follow-up interviews were carried out just under two years later, in 2004. Open ended questions were again used to investigate schools' progress with enterprise education and the changing attitudes and perceptions of staff.

This chapter sets out to show what we can learn from the ways in which Scottish schools seemed to be dealing with the dual agenda of enterprise and citizenship during this time of accelerated interest in both areas. In June 2004 the Scottish Executive produced an interim report about the apparent progress made with enterprise education in its *Determined to Succeed – One Year On* review document. Its ministerial foreword states:

> *DtS* goes to the heart of our vision for a smart, successful Scotland. Through it, we are helping to change the attitudes of our young people, so that they have a better chance of realising their full potential. We want to make sure they're better prepared – not just

for the world of work, whether in the private, public or voluntary sectors, but, more generally, for life. (Jim Wallace and Peter Peacock, quoted in Scottish Executive, 2004: ii)

We see how Scottish teachers were embracing this vision (see also Deuchar, 2006). Their views were captured at a time when the *DtS* agenda was first being introduced into schools and when education for citizenship had become a national priority in Scottish education.

Enterprising teachers, pupils and schools

The majority of teachers in the ten schools described enterprise in relation to the behaviour they associated with their own and colleagues' practice in the classroom. Teachers in four of the schools thought an enterprising teacher was one who could equip pupils with life skills and enable them to relate what they were learning to the outside world. Others thought it was a teacher who encouraged pupil responsibility in making decisions. Four teachers identified enterprising teachers as achieving the dual aims of developing pupil responsibility and relating their teaching to the outside world. One participant captured the way teachers were committed to empowering pupils to take responsibility but still found it challenging:

> I think it's more about letting go of the reins a bit as a teacher. I feel sometimes it's difficult for us to give the children real responsibility and I feel I'm getting closer to that now. *Class Teacher*

Teachers described the behaviour they would associate with an enterprising pupil in wide-ranging ways. For one class teacher an enterprising pupil was thoughtful, caring, kind to others and able to empathise but many talked more about individual children's ability to come up with new ideas, show confidence and lead and organise others (Deuchar, 2006):

> I'd probably use the words forward-thinking, somebody who had leadership skills but also somebody who was reasonably popular because to me an enterprising pupil has to be somebody that will work well with others. *Class Teacher*

Gradually teachers concentrated their concerns for enterprise on the need for social and moral responsibility, using this quality as a measure for enterprising behaviour in class. In one follow-up interview the class teacher appeared confident in her assessment of the growing nature of social responsibility among pupils (Deuchar, 2006):

> I think children working together is the key ... and being responsible for yourself ... I don't think children are as selfish as they were ten years ago. I think they think more about one another ... I think the collective responsibility of children is much greater than it was ten years ago. *Class Teacher*

Teachers also described enterprising behaviour in relation to their school as a whole. Two headteachers equated it to the number of enterprise projects in the school or the creation of a formal policy in enterprise education. But most staff referred to the participative and inclusive ethos in the school and the extent of autonomy granted to pupils for organising new initiatives and whole school events. Staff began to realise that the school could be classed as enterprising even if there were very few specific enterprise projects in place:

> It's not just the one class that do enterprise. I mean there's other children that are running things like an enterprise, because they go out and monitor the playground. *Headteacher*

> It's about mutual respect, the way people work together knowing you are as valued as the next person whether it's the janitor, the dinner lady, the headteacher, a pupil or whoever. *Headteacher*

Headteachers and class teachers were thus able to frame enterprising behaviour in terms of the teacher, pupil and school. Descriptions of it were wide-ranging. While some teachers felt that an enterprising teacher was one that afforded pupils responsibility and decision making skills, others related it to the ability to provide relevance in the curriculum and equip pupils for future life roles. This seemed to reflect the priorities set out in much of the documentation on enterprise education (Shuttleworth, 1993; Brownlow *et al*, 1998; Scottish Executive, 2002) as well as earlier thinking on the nature of enterprising teaching styles (Shacklock *et al*, 2000). Some teachers described enterprising behaviour in relation to pupils' confidence, ideas and skills at leading and managing others. Other teachers highlighted the need for teamwork and social responsibility towards peers. These mixed views seemed to reflect the essence of 'welfare liberalism' described by John Dewey (Fishman and McCarthy, 1998: 62), characterised by the honouring of both individual and collective priorities.

Over the research period, the teachers appeared to be responding to the wider policy changes focusing on social entrepreneurship and identified social and moral responsibility and selfless behaviour as a measure of enterprise (Scottish Executive, 2003a; LTScotland, 2002). Some headteachers reflected only upon the number of enterprise projects operating in the school or whether the school had a policy in enterprise education, while others measured an enterprising school according to the extent to which pupils were given responsibility and the valuing and respect of both staff and pupils. This holistic view of ethical enterprise lends itself to contemporary views of the active citizen, participating thoughtfully and responsibly in political, economic, social and cultural aspects of life (LTScotland, 2002).

Desired outcomes of enterprise education

Evidence from the interviews indicated how enterprise education was conceptualised in terms of desired outcomes. Some staff prioritised developing pupils' knowledge and understanding of the nature of business, how products can be marketed and sold, resources managed and profits used productively. Others considered it more important for pupils to develop core skills through enterprise, such as problem solving, working and communicating with others. Some staff advocated a change of approach away from enterprise education to the education of children to become enterprising people. Teachers related the latter approach with equipping pupils with more responsibility and helping them examine the need for interpersonal skills and social tolerance. Some teachers viewed the attitudes emerging from enterprise projects as most important. Some talked about the way projects could develop children's self-esteem. In some of the schools in socially deprived areas, staff related the outcomes of enterprise projects to the need to develop a culture enabling pupils to believe in their potential for contributing to society.

Many teachers also related the outcomes of enterprise education to enhanced motivation to learn and saw it as a means of improving attainment levels among pupils, particularly those they saw as low achievers. For instance, class teachers were impressed by how children became engaged when writing letters to local banks or businesses or writing reports about projects. Others described how enterprise education enabled pupils to develop skills in other areas of the curriculum, such as mathematics and expressive arts. And some noted how pupils worked more co-operatively and engaged in problem solving at a deeper level. A class teacher summed up like this:

> The main reason I started delivering enterprise projects years ago when it was probably unusual was because I thought it made things more meaningful ... more purpose. *Class Teacher*

In follow-up interviews, teachers in five of the schools confirmed their observations about the social benefits offered by enterprise and how it gave pupils confidence and maturity. They reported how less academically able pupils had the opportunity to achieve more and said that enterprise initiatives enabled teachers to provide a real and motivating context for learning. But they complained of the continuing pressure to meet externally imposed attainment targets and to cope with a crowded curriculum, which undermined their ability to engage in enterprise in its fullest sense. However, a head-teacher with a holistic approach to enterprise saw that enterprising approaches to teaching and learning were helping her school with the national attainment targets:

> I do think that the things we are doing by enabling and empowering the children is having a knock on effect on attainment ... the class teachers are doing many teaching developments in terms of independent learning and teaching the children about their personal learning ... so that is enterprising and that is giving them charge of their own learning ability to an extent. *Headteacher*

Staff expressed caution, however, about politicians' view of enterprise education as the universal remedy for all educational challenges. As one said:

> I have slight worries about the directions that come from the likes of Jack McConnell ... who seems to see enterprise as ... a panacea that's going to solve everything ... I think there are dangers that it could be seen to achieve more than it was actually ever geared to achieve. *Class Teacher*

Although teachers felt that the outcomes from enterprise could be wide and varied, they thought that children were less certain about this and tended to see it as fun and a way of making money:

> If you asked them, the first thing that would come into their mind would be 'we didn't do any work'. And then, if they were pushed, they would say that they raised money to give to charity. *Class Teacher*

Teachers viewed the learning outcomes of enterprise education in different ways. A minority regarded it solely as a means of enhancing pupils' knowledge of the world of work and introducing them to employment skills, risk taking and self-employment. But it seemed more common to frame the desired outcomes in terms of enhancing pupils' social and interpersonal skills, confidence, self-esteem and development of 'can do' attitudes. These views partly reflect the priorities set out by the Scottish Executive (2002: 6), which highlight the development of 'enterprising attitudes and skills' as a key priority. They also link strongly to the skills, competences, values and dispositions required for citizenship capability (LTScotland, 2002). However, the Scottish Executive's (2002: 6) references to other aims that would ensure pupils are prepared for 'innovation, wealth creation and entrepreneurship' featured less in the sample teachers' priorities.

Teachers appeared to regard enterprise as a great motivator, a way of making the curriculum real and of raising pupil attainment. Although the pressure of target-setting got in the way, some staff had a holistic view of enterprise and could recognise that enterprising approaches to teaching and learning were enabling pupils to meet those targets. They recognised that enterprise education was by no means a panacea and that pupils seldom recognised the learning achieved.

Business, community or environmental orientation

At first seven out of the ten schools delivered enterprise education solely through business-related projects. The pupils were introduced to the idea of a commercial company and took part in simulations involving advertising, finance, market research and sales. They were encouraged to design, make and market a new product in the school community and consider the options for profit making and managing resources. Teachers in these schools described how pupils were involved in writing to external companies and negotiating loans and in visiting local businesses to find out about profit making ventures. They invited business representatives in to talk to pupils about job applications and interviews.

Some schools viewed enterprise as a means of involving pupils in the community, encompassing some focus on the local and sometimes global environment. This might entail picking up litter in the local area, organising recycling activities and re-designing community gardens for the elderly. More challenging activities involved peer mediation schemes in the school playground or global initiatives to raise money for developing countries. In such cases teachers were clear about their aim of encouraging children to grow up to contribute towards the welfare of their own communities and the world at large.

The headteacher of one school talked at length about the work of pupil committees such as the Garden Gang and the Playground Improvement Group. Pupils had become involved in re-developing areas of the school grounds on a budget, drawing upon their own set of design ideas. Several schools had achieved their eco-schools award through innovation in local environmental activity and one had encouraged pupils to work with parents, teachers and members of the local community in devising a statement of shared values, which became the frame of reference for the school's code of conduct (see Case Study, Chapter 5).

During later interviews with staff it seemed that schools which had originally placed most emphasis on business-related themes were now evolving and expanding their practice into a social and community-based focus. Only a few schools did no more than business projects. But even in these schools the teachers also talked about other practices that enabled pupils to engage in decision making but were not necessarily classed as enterprise education.

Different schools placed emphasis on different educational priorities. The range of practice in the schools included setting up local and global campaigns, involving pupils in the participative decision making process through establishing committees that focused on environmental concerns and working with parents, staff and the local community. The evidence from this Scottish study suggests that the schools were generally moving towards a model of social entrepreneurship. This fitted the principles emerging from the renewed interest in citizenship education, with its emphasis on civic, political and social elements of learning (Marshall, 1950; QCA, 1998; Kerr, 1999; LTScotland, 2002). However, some schools did not always recognise that their generic practice in community involvement, pupil decision making and autonomous learning was directly related to the enterprise education agenda.

Communitarianism

As I dug deeper into Scottish teachers' responses to interview questions, more and more evidence emerged that illustrated that teachers located enterprise education as somewhere on a continuum between the traditional individualistic view of business entrepreneurship and the more collectivist view of social entrepreneurship. Illustrations of the way teachers' views could be clustered in each part of this continuum are now examined.

Individualism

One set of responses provided a range of ideas associated with the Thatcherite view of entrepreneurship: individualism, self-interest and personal ambition. For example, we saw that some teachers spoke about the need for pupils to emerge from enterprise projects with a solid understanding of how a company operates and how to make money. Others expressed their desired outcomes from enterprise initiatives in terms of equipping pupils with the skills to market and sell themselves and for pupils to become confident, mature and responsible.

Many teachers framed their definitions of an enterprising pupil in terms of individualistic qualities such as confidence, determination, resilience and the ability to organise and lead others. One head-teacher clearly felt comfortable with including aspects of competition within the school curriculum while another talked about the danger of under-playing profit making within projects:

> We have to be very careful that we are not having any negative views of profit, because we don't make a profit. We're salaried public servants ... I do think it's important that we don't just give a very cosy, caring message and not an accurate account. *Head-teacher*

These responses illustrate that teachers felt that some form of individualistic emphasis within enterprise was to be expected and that this should, to some extent, be reflected within an enterprise education programme. Some were enthusiastic about pupils learning about the needs of business, being trained to sell themselves and to develop ambition, determination and the will to persevere. Other teachers felt comfortable with introducing children to the competitive side of enterprise and valued the inclusion of profit-making ventures.

Collectivism

Some teachers in the study associated enterprise activities with enabling pupils to work in teams and come up with collective responses. In one case the headteacher noted how enterprise initiatives could be used to harmonise the tensions between specific pupils:

> The enterprise project served to reunite the children and to bring them together and to work towards a common goal and to bury their differences. *Headteacher*

This view of enterprise education as a means of social cohesion was not uncommon. Other teachers talked about the need for promoting collectivist values as a means of preparation for life and work:

> I think working in teams and co-operation is the most important thing. I know from friends and family who are involved in commerce and industry that's what they're looking for ... if you are an absolute swine of a person who is going to cause mayhem on a staff they don't want to know. *Headteacher*

Some teachers spoke about the need for pupils to use their initiative to further the goals of the local community, and charitable causes were seen as important end results of fundraising activities. Some staff identified the focus on co-operative skills and teamwork, the need to value other people's contributions and to show respect for them. Some talked about the need for inter-class co-operation so that pupils supported each other in whole school activities.

There was plenty of evidence of teachers' perceived connections between enterprise and collectivism and the ways collectivist ideals could emerge from enterprise education. Many teachers spoke about the strong parallels between enterprising behaviour and the need to care for others, co-operate and work for charitable causes. Some teachers appeared to see this as good preparation for the world of working in industry, where employers were keen to have staff who could work well with others and value their relationships with colleagues.

Representing the third way

The need for mixing compassion and ethics with ambition, innovation, self-interest and wealth creation was also illustrated by teachers in the study. Their views reflected a form of communitarianism with a focus on both social and economic enterprise. Some class teachers identified pupils who displayed insight into the expression of their own goals and also sensitivity towards including others and promoting a team ethic. Others described recent enterprise projects in terms of dual aims, which centred upon developing pupils' knowledge of business along with the inclusion of personal and social development and a strong community focus. One class teacher described the activities involved in her enterprise project in terms of handling finance but also of being socially and morally mindful with its management in the community:

> We speak about why we would charge less to old people, we have to look at people's incomes ... would children pay less than an adult for the ticket? We talked about prices and what would be reasonable because a lot of the senior citizens come free. *Class Teacher*

By the end of the study, teachers' views were centred upon more holistic endeavours such as pupil councils, with dual aims of enabling pupils not only to raise money but to use it to improve school resources and to help others. Some teachers expressed their desired outcomes from enterprise education in terms of instilling the notion of rights and responsibilities. Others went further in their uniting of seemingly opposing educational values such as ambition, determination and risk taking with tolerance, interdependence, compassion and respect. Some included a global element to projects, as one response illustrates (Deuchar, 2006):

> I suppose the recycled card in a way is making them look at ... a global situation and the Thailand challenge is making them look at a global situation... and perhaps out of that you might start to look at ... fair trade companies. *Class Teacher*

Some of the teachers who had taught enterprise for a while were concluding that there were children in every class who gravitated towards either collectivism or self-interest. One teacher mentioned pupils who tended to overlook other people's feelings in their decisions and displayed attitudes associated with 'the typical hard-nosed businessman'. The headteacher from this school agreed, but pointed out that other children tended to concentrate too much on the needs of others and that maybe both kinds of values were needed (Deuchar, 2006):

> Within every given class you get the whole spectrum. You see the ruthless, cut-throat person ... you'll get the children who put their own needs second ... it's probably quite useful to assess those as two separate things: when is the child focusing on their own development of skills and the product and objectives? When are they supporting others and being a carer within the group, or acknowledging other people's needs? And when is one at the detriment of the other? *Headteacher*

Many teachers saw enterprise and the outcomes of enterprise education in terms of the dual perspectives of individual values as well as social and ethical priorities. They focused on maintaining a strong element of business-related knowledge, enabling pupils to set goals while incorporating aspects of profit making and competition. They thought that business knowledge should be mixed with strong civic awareness, individual goal setting with team ethics and that a charitable focus should be part of profit making ventures.

Concern about collective responsibility was a growing priority of many of the schools. More projects involved global awareness, eco-schools initiatives and peer mediation and community involvement. Teachers sought a balance between promoting self-interest and sentiment in any enterprise endeavour.

The findings from the study show that seemingly opposing agendas were often comfortably reconciled. The schools were encouraging pupils to recognise what they were learning in terms of their own personal goals and of their commitment to serving other people. Teachers often viewed enterprise in relation to communitarian principles, reflecting values associated with New Labour's third way, and the political and cultural expectations being placed on schools to represent a reconciliation of neo-liberal enterprise with social justice and ethics (Fairclough, 2000; Davies *et al*, 2001). A minority of teachers continued to define enterprise solely in terms of themes associated with the neo-liberal agenda.

Summary

This chapter has presented the data emerging from a small sample of Scottish headteacher and class teacher interviews about their views on enterprising behaviour and the purpose of enterprise education. The main findings are summarised as follows:

- ▧ Over the course of the study many teachers' attitudes towards enterprise were widening and the focus on projects was being replaced by a more holistic view of enterprising teaching styles.

- ▧ There was a developing emphasis on the need to instil social and moral responsibility through enterprise education. A popular view was to see enterprise as being framed between self-interest and ethics; many teachers recognised the need for rights as well as responsibilities, ambition as well as tolerance and wealth creation as well as charity.

- ▧ Although the attainment agenda was seen as a pressure, teachers were increasingly finding that a more holistic view of enterprising teaching, with a focus on pupil consultation, allowed them to address wider attainment targets.

The teachers' views seemed to match the rhetoric of New Labour's third way, which combines a focus on economic dynamism with social justice (Fairclough, 2000). Enterprise was gradually redefined in many teachers' minds as a means of promoting the newer priorities associated with the citizenship agenda.

Pause for reflection

The nature of pupils' experience of enterprise education depends greatly on the way in which teachers, student teachers and policy makers view the agenda themselves. By completing the exercise below you can identify the extent to which you prioritise individualistic perspectives, collectivist perspectives or a mixture of both. The principles identified as most important could form the basis of a school project or a policy statement in enterprise education. A strong emphasis on both individualism and collectivist outcomes would enhance the potential for dovetailing enterprise education with education for citizenship.

Listed below are some reasons for providing pupils with enterprise education activities. Identify how important you think each reason is:

	Not at all important	Not very important	Fairly important	Very important
■ To give pupils an opportunity to find out more about the world of work				
■ To enhance employability skills				
■ To develop personal transferable skills				
■ To introduce pupils to the ideas of self-employment				
■ To enable pupils to learn about the key aspects of running a business				
■ To enable pupils to create an idea and make a financial profit				

	Not at all important	Not very important	Fairly important	Very important
■ To develop individual goal-setting				
■ To develop pupils' persuasive powers				
■ To enable pupil participation in running the school				
■ To develop risk-taking skills				
■ To develop pupils' awareness of human rights				
■ To develop pupils' understanding of community structures				
■ To empower pupils to develop informed environmental attitudes				
■ To develop team-work and communication among pupils				
■ To develop knowledge about social issues and dilemmas				
■ To develop consultation between staff and pupils				
■ To prepare pupils for adult roles, such as parent, partner, colleague				
■ To enable pupils to become lifelong learners				
■ To enable pupils to become thoughtful and responsible citizens				
■ To enhance pupils' political awareness				
■ To develop pupils' moral considerations when making decisions				
■ As a means of motivating pupils				
■ To help raise attainment				
■ To make the curriculum more meaningful and real				
■ To enhance self-awareness and self-esteem				

4

'Lull them into a false sense of security, then hit them with the double-glazing bit!': pupils' responses to the enterprise agenda

A rguably education can be characterised as a 'moral enterprise', with the aim of helping young people to live better individual lives and to encourage them to contribute towards wider society (Davies, 2002: 113). In such terms, enterprise education needs to be viewed by pupils in our schools as being about more than developing personal ambition and the determination to succeed in business. It needs to include aspects of civic, republican and liberal objectives (Heater, 1999; Davies, 2002). Enterprise and citizenship discourse is co-joined in many of the learning outcomes and suggested activities in both the English national curriculum and the Scottish national guidelines. The Scottish Executive (2002) argues that the values and dispositions desirable as outcomes from enterprise education overlap with those identified for education for citizenship. This chapter builds upon the evidence of teachers' views and draws upon the responses of sample groups of pupils from each of the ten focus schools described in chapter 3. It illustrates pupils' perceptions about enterprising behaviour and explores pupils' views on enterprise education and its connection with communitarian principles.

The sample group

As in chapter 3, the research was conducted within a range of primary schools set within a variety of socio-economic backgrounds. The pupils, who were all in P4, P5 or P6 classes (ages 8-10) during the initial stages of the research in 2002, completed written questionnaires and small samples of pupils also participated in group discussions. I tracked samples of pupils as they progressed through primary school and gleaned additional information from pupil questionnaires and discussion groups in 2003 when pupils were in P5, P6 or P7 (ages 9-11). I was able to track pupils again, following their progression through primary school or their transition to secondary education in 2004 when they were in P6, P7 or Secondary 1 (S1) (ages10-12).

This chapter reports on the evidence of pupils' views which emerged from the three phases of the research. It illustrates their values and attitudes in relation to enterprise education and the way it might connect with citizenship. Davies (2002) is clear about the difference between broad and narrow forms of enterprise education and its relationship to citizenship:

> If one sees it as relating only to economic matters and requiring a suspension of critical thinking then it is unhelpful. If, on the other hand, enterprise is seen as requiring a broader perspective that implies a willingness and ability to be innovative in many different ways and contexts within a democratic framework then it may relate very positively to valuable forms of citizenship. (Davies, 2002: 124)

This chapter illustrates the extent to which the sample pupils viewed enterprise in this more holistic way.

Pupil definitions of the entrepreneur

In early questionnaires, pupils were asked to provide their own meaning of enterprise and to name people that they thought were enterprising. They were also asked to provide examples of enterprising qualities and to provide cartoon drawings of entrepreneurs. In discussion groups, a cross-section of pupils expanded and developed their ideas. Evidence in this section builds and extends outcomes already reported in previous publications by the author (Deuchar, 2004; 2006).

Family members were described as enterprising in almost all of the schools because they were seen as helpful and encouraged children to resolve disagreements with their brothers or sisters. Friends were cited for coming up with ideas, for persevering, or because they were fun to be around. Pupils in two of the sample schools selected their teacher or headteacher. In one school pupils regarded their headteacher as enterprising because she created good ideas such as establishing new initiatives to help people in the local community, and setting up the pupil council. The most popular choice of sports personality among pupils was David Beckham. Pupils admired his capacity for teamwork, entertainment and creating ideas:

> He's got his own brand of clothes. And he's constantly thinking up new ways to beat people ... tricks that he can make up ... he's very enterprising in his hairstyles. *Andrew, P6 boy*

Some pupils felt that pop stars were enterprising because they worked collectively and created new ideas. Children in four of the schools talked about historical figures, such as Alexander Graham Bell or Nelson Mandela, while pupils in two schools referred to political figures such as Tony Blair and George Bush. However, while the pupils felt that both Bush and Blair were confident and courageous, they also disliked Bush's hankering for power and Blair's tendency to follow where Bush led. These views were emerging at the time of the Iraq war of 2003, and pupils were clearly reflecting upon the political stories in the media at this time (see chapter 6 for further evidence of this). Pupils in only three schools referred to business entrepreneurs such as Richard Branson and Bill Gates. Some pupils talked about their ability to create new ventures and to ensure that these projects expanded and developed.

Pupils were asked to make cartoon drawings of entrepreneurs and to describe the main qualities they associated with them. In all ten of the sample schools pupils thought that enterprising people needed to be caring, since this quality was useful when creating new ideas or participating in fundraising:

> I drew the lady in some of the shops ... she has a can and shakes it. Children come up with money and she gives them a sticker at the end ... for cancer research ... people can die from cancer and she's trying to keep them alive. *Jenna, P5 girl*

55

Pupils also saw the importance of teamwork and co-operation and thought that you could achieve more by working with others than by working on your own. However, some pupils also associated enterprising behaviour with qualities such as confidence and ambition. Some pupils saw courage as important and referred to explorers who sailed around the world to achieve their lifelong goals. Pupils also felt that entrepreneurs needed to be dynamic to succeed with new ideas but also to be flexible if they didn't succeed the first time round. They also saw the importance of risk taking and goal setting. Pupils in two schools associated an enterprising person with the ability to be shrewd, cunning and ruthless:

> You need to be able to get the person to co-operate ... to be friendly, and then lull them into a false sense of security and then hit them with the double-glazing bit. *Neil, P6 boy*

Pupils in four of the schools talked about combining individualism, compassion and morality. For example, some liked the idea that Bill Gates gave £400 million to a global programme to vaccinate children against deadly diseases and felt that this made him more enterprising (Deuchar, 2005). Indeed, this was not a unique view; other pupils talked about footballers who made a great deal of money but also had ethical values, such as Peter Lovenkrands who made donations to charity and David Beckham who spent money on his children and also donated to the tsunami disaster appeal. It seems that some pupils were developing a capacity to hold dual images of prominent figures from the world of business and entertainment in their minds. The media was clearly having an influence here and Tom Hunter's model of charitable entrepreneurship was obviously having an impact on pupils' values (Deuchar, 2005; 2006).

Following their transition to secondary school pupils were asked again to talk about enterprising behaviour and come up with specific examples. Their ideas had clearly expanded: in one school, pupils referred to Jesus because of the sacrifices he had made for humanity. Others referred to charities such as the Scottish Catholic International Aid Fund (SCIAF). Some pupils talked about examples of creativity from developing countries:

> African people .... They use their initiative to build their houses, be-
> cause they've got to plan out the whole thing and they've got to use
> mud and stuff like that. Then they've got to bake it in the sun.
> Honestly, I really do think that African people use their initiative in
> a good way and they also use teamwork to build this. *Thomas, S1
> pupil*

Responses of this kind were fairly common among pupils and many of them seemed to be developing more of a global perspective. One pupil also felt that arrogance was needed in order to be successful:

> If they're not going to be a wee bit cocky they're going to be dead
> shy and they're not going to be able to show their real selves. *Gary,
> S1 boy*

The pupils' ideas thus fitted into both ends of the communitarian continuum. Many pupils felt that enterprising individuals had good ideas for helping other people, worked well with others and had tolerance and respect for cultural and community diversity (LTScotland, 2002). Others felt that enterprising people needed determination, competitive spirit and creativity. These ideas reflected HMIE's (2004) and LTScotland's (2002) focus on independent creativity and the ability to make informed decisions. As pupils moved from primary to secondary education their references to the modern thrusting entrepreneur model and the need for economic enterprise continued to be rare but now widened to include some more charitable causes, religious references and multicultural perspectives.

This continued focus on collectivist principles combined with new perspectives on cosmopolitan pluralism seemed to reflect the social orientation associated with many teachers' views of citizenship (Davies *et al*, 1999; Potter, 2002). While a minority of pupils continued to associate enterprise with ruthless and cunning behaviour, more reflective participants felt that money-making projects should have a charitable focus. This seemed to reflect the current political rhetoric of combining economic restoration with cultural and moral regeneration (Fairclough, 2000; Loxley and Thomas, 2001).

Pupil views on enterprising jobs
During the second phase of the study, pupils in P5-7 classes (ages 9-11) were asked to identify jobs on a given list that they associated

with enterprising behaviour. Pupils felt that company directors, headteachers, scientists, artists, teachers and lawyers could be enterprising but were less sure about manual jobs such as lorry drivers, cleaners, waiters, labourers, janitors and joiners. In follow-up discussion groups, pupils debated these views. As a result of this debate pupils were more able to see how enterprise could be applied to the world of work in a general sense, rather than merely within professional or self-employment contexts. The following extracts of discussion and debate illustrate this well:

John: I don't think a lorry driver could be enterprising. You don't need to be enterprising to drive!

Lewis: You could think of the routes you have to do and take short-cuts.

Vicky: Yeah, they need to be enterprising because they need to make sure they have enough rests between the journeys.

Suzy: A waiter or waitress isn't enterprising because all they do is serve food.

Faiza: They could be funny ... a friendly attitude ... like TGI Friday's: they all dress up in wacky clothes, they do face paints and go behind the bar and chuck up bottles.

Anna: A cleaner isn't enterprising because all they do is just clean up.

Thomas: They can be enterprising because they're talking to people in the houses as well. They could set up their own business.

Aarif: Yeah, they've got to make the streets clean for other people so they're helping other people and they're doing a dirty job which isn't exactly the best job to have and they're doing it for other people.

Jane: I don't think a builder is enterprising.

Taylor: I disagree. You probably need to talk to people as well and you need to be pretty brave. What if you've done all the roof and then the roof accidentally falls. That's a wee bit of a risk to their lives!

Sam: I don't think a janitor is enterprising because there's not many ways that you can clean up rubbish.

Kirsty: But they make the school and playground safe. They make sure no one could get in that would harm us.

Matthew: A headteacher isn't enterprising because headteachers don't work very much.

Saaib: I disagree because headteachers have good ideas ... ways to stop bullying, ways to be kind and helpful to each another ... getting stuff for the playground.

One pupil summed up the views when he mentioned that in fact you could be enterprising in any job. A particularly reflective pupil felt that it depended on whether you looked at it from a business sense or a community sense, but that enterprise could be applied to any occupation. There were many indications that the pupils' initial ideas about the world of work were expanding. They gradually came to see that any job could be carried out in an enterprising way by making extra efforts and being innovative. For example, pupils talked about entertaining people and providing more of a service for people. These views were reflective of the libertarian view of work proposed by Chomsky (1988) and Corson (1988), built upon the Marxist perspective of seeing work as a free and conscious activity. The pupils gradually began to see the need for innovation and entre-preneurial zeal in the world of work (Shuttleworth, 1993). These views were consonant with LTScotland's (2002) view of the need for pupils to become active citizens through making the best use of their own creative abilities.

Perceived outcomes from enterprise education

The sample pupils initially saw enterprise education in terms of business-related projects in school and associated it with money making ventures. In the majority of schools pupils described how they had made something to sell within the school community and had been introduced to advertising, marketing and finance. Some pupils talked specifically about the way in which they had learned about calculating projected profits. The pupils also felt that they had learned about taking responsibility, working with others and the im-portance of listening to other people's points of view. Pupils in one school had been involved in an environmentally-based enterprise project where they re-designed the school playground and felt that they had learned about the importance of looking after their local community.

The most common enterprise projects were centred on buying and selling, making, designing and managing. In some schools pupils set up gift shops; in others they designed pupil badges and created Christmas gift tags, tea towels or fridge magnets. In one school pupils were involved in team building exercises at a supported study group and felt that this was an enterprising way of learning:

> We've been doing team work – we go into groups and do the team challenges. Stuff you have to work out in your team ... you pick people in your team to do exercises. *Steven, P7 boy*

Another school had established a football coaching company: older pupils were responsible for coaching younger pupils in exchange for a small fee. Pupils took up roles such as managing director, advertising manager and head coach. There was also a team of assistant coaches. As a result of this project those pupils who previously associated enterprise solely with business now saw the importance of helping others and working in the community.

During follow-up visits to schools in early 2004, the majority of pupils had transferred to secondary education. They were asked to indicate the type of learning they most valued from enterprise projects from a given list. Almost half of the pupils identified teamwork and listening to others as an important learning outcome, while just over one third of pupils regarded taking responsibility and discussion as important. The least commonly chosen outcomes included the ability to be in charge of a project and to become involved in managing finances (Brownlow *et al*, 2004).

However, some pupils also thought that it was important to learn about finance at the same time as learning about teamwork and co-operation. In the words of one pupil, 'you need to work as a group to get somewhere and you also need money'. Indeed, pupils in two schools continued to see enterprise education as a means of learning about commercial success:

> Being an entrepreneur, making your own things and selling it and making a business out of it ... making money, maybe starting your own business. *Samantha, S1 girl; Aadil, S1 boy*

Pupils talked about the type of enterprise education they had experienced since moving to secondary school. This included creating a class magazine in English, making a poster about natural disasters for geography, participating in group discussions in English and a court simulation exercise in modern studies. In one school pupils had been involved in a whole school event when they organised a coffee morning for the elderly, while another group of students had participated in a collaborative challenge as part of their S1 welcome day. Pupils in all schools could describe at least one teacher who was enterprising, although they often referred back to their primary teachers:

> Miss Cameron and Miss Hill... they're practically alike because they're both funny and they both take ideas from kids. *Jack, S1 boy*

Some interesting perspectives emerged from pupils over the three years of the research project. Their perceptions about enterprise education were initially framed around a capitalist model, incorporating elements of profit making, finance and sales. While this seemed to relate to that part of the current policy agenda that focuses on independent creativity, career development and wealth creation (LTScotland, 2002; HMIE, 2004), it was less reflective of the other recognised priorities for civic engagement (LTScotland, 2002).

Once pupils were engaged in the projects they understood the importance of teamwork, listening to others and taking collective responsibility. In many cases they were participating in business-related projects. Some pupils were involved in more innovative projects where enterprise was seen in a broad sense, with a focus on community service and team building. In such cases pupils' views about enterprise were redefined to incorporate capability for citizenship, based on aspects of civic engagement.

Following their transition to secondary school, pupils' participation in enterprise education diminished. Apart from a few isolated instances they had not engaged in enterprise activities since leaving primary school. However, their ideas about enterprise were still sharp: although it was more common for pupils to identify collectivist values as the most important to emerge from enterprise projects, a minority highlighted the value of learning about finance, making money, taking risks and preparing to set up your own business.

The Scottish Executive's (2002) aims of instilling positive attitudes in pupils towards becoming successful employees, employers and entrepreneurs were clearly prevalent. However, pupils were also able to reflect upon the social and moral values needed for a place in society and highlighted in the recent priorities for citizenship education (QCA, 1998; LTScotland, 2002). Although many of their ideas about enterprise were widening due to their primary education experiences, their experiences were more limited following their transition to secondary school.

Summary

This chapter has highlighted the changing and evolving views of Scottish pupils about enterprising behaviour and the purpose of enterprise education. The main findings are summarised as follows:

- Pupils most commonly associated enterprising behaviour with family members, friends and personalities from the world of entertainment and politics.

- Only a few pupils felt that enterprising people were driven solely by selfish motives or the need to create personal wealth. Many associated enterprise with social and moral values although some identified the need to combine ego-centrism with a drive to fulfil their duties to others.

- Pupils gradually began to feel that you could be creative and enterprising in any job, not just in those associated with self-employment or the professions. These views seemed to reflect current political thinking that has been channelled into recent national policy on both enterprise and citizenship education.

- Primary schools took a more holistic view of enterprise education and embedded it into much of their wider practice although pupils tended to associate the word 'enterprise' with specific school projects.

- Pupils' experience of enterprise diminished as they transferred to secondary education and S1 pupils often talked about projects and innovations they had experienced in primary school.

The last two chapters have provided insight into teachers' and pupils' views about enterprising behaviour, enterprise education and links with the citizenship agenda. The communitarian attitudes and values that were emerging among Scottish teachers and pupils have been identified. This leads on to the examination of specific examples of how pupils can be given opportunities for creativity, enterprise and active citizenship through democratic participation in school. The following two chapters open this analysis.

Pause for reflection
It might be useful to establish the qualities and jobs that you associate with enterprise, and the extent to which these relate to capitalist and/or ethical and social contexts. The two exercises on page 64 provide a way of exploring this. The exercises could be turned into a debate, with the qualities and jobs presented on cards and used as a stimulus for discussion with colleagues. As a team you could explore whether you associate enterprise solely with business and individualism, or whether you see it as more closely related to wider innovation in a range of social contexts. The outcomes of your discussion could form the basis of a policy statement on enterprise. Depending on the outcomes of your discussion, you may be able to align the focus on enterprise education with a focus on citizenship.

Identify the qualities that you think describes someone who is enterprising:

rich	☐	caring	☐	ordinary	☐
sensitive	☐	clever	☐	visionary	☐
creative	☐	responsible	☐	political	☐
confident	☐	determined	☐	independent	☐
takes risks	☐	ambitious	☐	team player	☐
selfish	☐	greedy	☐	leader	☐
enthusiastic	☐	respectful	☐	poor	☐
friendly	☐	unusual	☐	arrogant	☐

Identify the jobs that you think people can be enterprising in –

director	☐	cleaner	☐	accountant	☐
janitor	☐	engineer	☐	headteacher	☐
scientist	☐	footballer	☐	office worker	☐
teacher	☐	waiter/waitress	☐	electrician	☐
builder	☐	politician	☐	labourer	☐
artist	☐	lawyer	☐	journalist	☐
doctor	☐	lorry driver	☐	joiner	☐
nurse	☐	fire fighter	☐	secretary	☐

Enterprising Citizens

- Who is in the picture you have drawn ? _Mum_

- Why did you choose to draw this person ? _because she_ _uses her skills to help people._

- What does the person do that is enterprising ? _She works_ _hard and helps people._

Enterprising Citizens

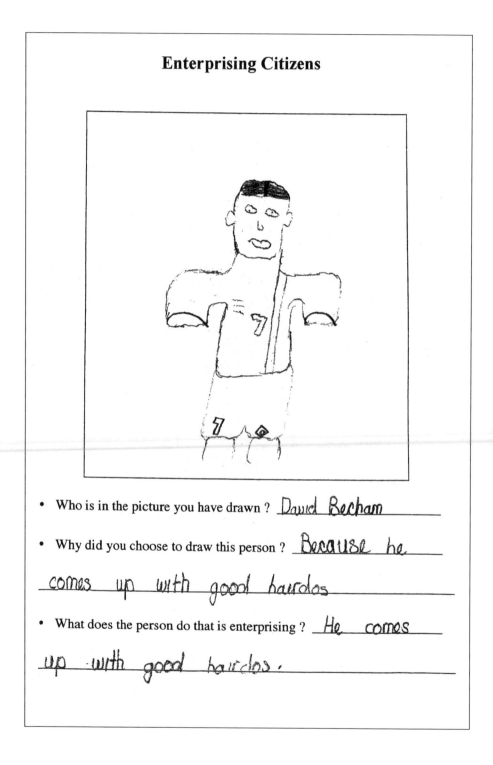

- Who is in the picture you have drawn ? _David Becham_

- Why did you choose to draw this person ? _Because he comes up with good hairdos_

- What does the person do that is enterprising ? _He comes up with good hairdos._

66

Enterprising Citizens

- Who is in the picture you have drawn ? Richard Branson

- Why do you think this person is enterprising ? It is because
he came up with all the different
ideas of virgin

Enterprising Citizens

- **Who is in the picture you have drawn ?** _Paula (friend)_

- **Why do you think this person is enterprising ?** _I picked_
Paula because she always has
good ideas and talks out loud.

5

Creating a democratic culture: the role of pupil councils

C hapter 2 pointed to the international evidence that schools are still hierarchical in structure and that classrooms still tend to be dominated by authoritarian approaches to teaching. This conflicts with the principles underpinning the enterprise and citizenship agendas, which encourage pupils' active participation in their own learning. Schools need to implement pupil-led agendas which encourage personal ambition and determination but also enable children to consider contemporary social and global issues. This chapter examines the potential of pupil councils for creating a democratic school ethos which enables children to become enterprising in both a business and social context and to engage in active, responsible citizenship.

Pupil councils: the pros and cons
As discussed briefly in chapter 1, the UN Convention on the Rights of the Child highlights the need for children to have freedom of expression, develop civic identity and have the opportunity to become active citizens:

Article 12: The right to freely express an opinion in all matters affecting him/her and to have that opinion taken into account.

Article 14: The right to meet together with other children and join and form associations.

Article 29:   The right to an education which prepares her/him for an active responsible life as an adult in a free society.

(UN General Assembly, 1989: articles 12-29)

Pupil councils may play an important role in enabling the realisation of these rights. They may provide a vehicle for pupils to see the worth of what they are learning in terms of their own personal goals and of their commitment to serving other people (Deuchar, 2004).

Pupil councils have long been recognised as a means of enabling pupils to engage in responsible and active citizenship, as well as learning about democratic values. The Taylor Committee of Inquiry into School Government recommended that secondary pupils should participate in managing schools, although schools were initially left to develop their own ideas on an *ad hoc* basis (Baginsky and Hannam, 1999). The Elton Report of 1989 recommended the use of pupil councils as a vehicle for improving pupil motivation but progress was hampered by the introduction of the national curriculum in England and Wales and the 5-14 guidelines in Scotland. It has been argued that these initiatives led to an overloaded and prescriptive curriculum that made it more difficult for teachers to become responsive to pupils' ideas. Nevertheless, both the Advisory Group on Citizenship (QCA, 1998) and its Scottish equivalent (LT-Scotland, 2002) have endorsed the need for fully functioning pupil councils:

> Pupil participation should be developed within a framework that ... devolves the process of decision making on the responsible uses of resources, for example those that have been allocated to pupil councils. (LT Scotland, 2002: 15)

Dobie (1998) argues that these councils can play a huge role in encouraging pupils to have a sense of ownership in the life of the school community. Taking part in such councils enables pupils to develop a range of attributes such as taking account of other points of view, working as part of a team and taking responsibility for decision making (Dobie, 1998). Baginsky and Hannam (1999: iii) argue that pupil councils are an effective way of signalling to students that they are respected and that 'their capacity to contribute to the task of school improvement is recognised.' They cite the School Council UK's view that the councils give pupils the opportunity to:

- participate in shaping and reviewing the school's behaviour policy, based upon finding non-violent ways of resolving conflict

- realise that they have a positive role to play in caring for each other and to assist in dealing with issues such as bullying and eliminating discrimination

- be involved in the caring process in school and the development of self-confidence, self-esteem, mutual respect, self-discipline and social responsibility.

(Baginsky and Hannam, 1999: iii)

Taylor and Johnson (2002: 2) argue that pupil councils can contribute to the development of pupils' social and moral responsibility, community involvement and political literacy, thereby addressing 'the three main strands of citizenship education.' International research suggests that councils should awaken pupils' motivation to engage with the exercising of rights and responsibilities in everyday life, offer children responsibility for service in the community and promote positive behaviour (Halstead and Taylor, 2000; Taylor and Johnston, 2002).

Positive evidence of success in this field comes from the Nordic countries. The Danish Education Act 1996 creates a statutory requirement for secondary schools to create pupil councils. Documentation that sets out the rights and responsibilities of pupils to manage their own representative bodies has also been released in Norway, Austria, Belgium, Cyprus, France, Spain and Portugal (Baginsky and Hannam, 1999). This reflects the wider development of international structures that aim to involve young people in political decision making, such as the European Youth Parliament, National Youth Parliaments in the Caribbean and New Zealand, as well as the more localised structures in cities across Europe (Burke and Grosvenor, 2003). In Britain, Blair's government created a new Cabinet Committee for Children and Young People in 2000, which was combined with the creation of the Scottish Youth Parliament and Scottish Civic Forum in Scotland.

However, it is essential that pupil councils are not tokenistic. Baginsky and Hannam (1999: iii) highlight the fact that the agendas associated with many councils tend not to roam far outside the 'charmed circle of lockers, dinners and uniform'. They call for wider issues to be discussed that involve the pupils in genuine discussion and debate over serious educational issues, guided by the creation of a democratic climate:

> it takes time and very careful preparation to build a climate in which both teachers and students feel comfortable in working to-gether on a constructive review of aspects of teaching, learning and schooling ... If the school is not ready for student participation then a school council can become a way of formalising and chan-nelling students' criticisms – an exercise in damage limitation rather than an opportunity for constructive consultation. (Baginsky and Hannam, 1999: iii)

A pupil council can become tokenistic if teachers only pay lip service to pupils' views and suggestions or where serious issues are side-stepped and the school hierarchy remains unchallenged. Alderson (2000) provides evidence that less than one fifth of pupils surveyed described their pupil council as effective. While Taylor and Johnston (2002) report many positive illustrations in primary schools, they also describe less favourable views emerging from secondary schools. Often this is because the power of the school hierarchy leads to student apathy. Research indicates that many pupil councils tend to focus merely on Baginsky and Hannam's (1999: iii) aptly named 'charmed circle' of dinners, school uniforms and playground issues, while more serious educational issues remain absent from the agendas:

> In the majority of schools, discussion of larger, serious issues, such as school development planning, teaching approaches or even staff appointments, was conspicuous by its absence on pupil council agendas. (Deuchar, 2004a: 164)

Pupil councils are clearly recognised as a vehicle for personal and social development and active citizenship in schools. They have potential for developing multi-faceted skills, values and qualities. They can encourage pupils to value other people's views, to give them the opportunity to shape school policy and to enable them to become actively involved in their local community. Lessons have clearly been learned from the Nordic countries where statutory requirements for creating pupil councils are well established. However, questions remain over the type of current educational practice that surrounds pupil councils.

Case studies of practice in primary schools

From the wider sample of Scottish schools described in previous chapters, a sub-set of five primary schools which were known to have well-established pupil councils was explored. While two of the schools were in highly affluent and quite rural areas, two others were located in inner city settings with mixed social backgrounds. The fifth school was in an extremely deprived area with a high level of drug-related crime. They varied in their ethnic make up: one school contained a high majority of ethnic minority pupils but the others had predominantly white pupil populations.

Between 2002 and 2003, pupil council meetings were observed in each of the five schools using semi-structured observation schedules, based on previous research by Taylor and Johnson (2002). The aim was to explore the way in which pupil members represented the school population, the type of items discussed and the style of interaction that emerged. Follow-up interviews were conducted with the teachers who led the pupil councils, the pupil members and children from the wider school populations. The purpose was to explore the pupils' and teachers' perceived aims for the council, the evidence of pupil learning and the impact of the councils on the schools. The case study in box 5.1 gives an overview of the pupil council's work in one of the inner city primary schools in the sample.

Box 5.1: Case study of a primary school pupil council

The pupil council in this large primary school, located within a fairly mixed socio-economic background and with a large ethnic minority pupil body, has been in place for four years. The school has routine fortnightly meetings in which representatives from primary 1 to primary 7 get together with their headteacher to discuss the various points on their agenda. The agenda is informed by the

---

outcomes of various class meetings and also from matters raised by the eco-school committee, litter committee and gardening committee. At one particular meeting, items include the need to organise fruit for the new healthy tuckshop, the selection and costing of new games to be introduced into each school classroom and the debate about how to prevent P7 boys from ruining new plants in the playground during recreational football games. In addition, pupil members from the eco-school committee report on their progress in finding a 'safe way to school' route for young pupils and their intentions to begin trying to solve the problem of double-parking outside the school. The gardening committee members also report on their progress with planting new seeds in the school grounds.

The council members talk about their progress in devising a statement of 'shared values' in collaboration with teachers, parents and members of the local community. This will later form the basis of the school's new 'code of conduct'. One value will underpin all the school's ongoing Personal and Social Development topics each month and will also be the focus of the school's monthly class assemblies where pupils from each class will talk to the school about the work they have been doing to promote the value. Values identified so far include honesty, respect and multi-cultural awareness. The latter is seen as particulary important because of the school's large population of children from ethnic minority groups, and the recent enrolment of 25 Slovakian pupils. The headteacher acts as facilitator during the meeting, inviting members of sub-committees to give reports and pupils to give feedback to new suggestions. Where appropriate, she also makes suggestions or provides relevant information. The pupils take the lead in the discussion and are able to speak at any time. One member of the council acts as chairperson and one other member acts as secretary. At the end of their meeting pupils decide to make an announcement at the next school assembly about the new healthy tuckshop, to organise the distribution of new games to classrooms and to monitor the football situation in the playground. Council members are reminded by the headteacher that class meetings should take place next week and items raised will form the agenda for the next council meeting. Other committees will also continue their work and bring updates to the next meeting.

Although committed to the idea of the pupil council, some teachers in the school can be more efficient than others at organising class meetings in the weeks between council meetings. Pupils are elected to the council by strong democratic means: pupils in each class who wish to stand prepare a manifesto and poster, the school population votes in proper polling stations and an election count takes place. Children who are on the council feel that it provides an opportunity for their voices to be heard, enables them to make changes in the school and helps everyone to feel happy and proud of their achievements. Non-council members also seem happy about the process, although some felt disappointed about not being elected. Many changes have come about as a result of the pupil council, such as the introduction of new water coolers in the school, plants in the playground and new games for recreational use. The headteacher sees the pupil council as an important means of hearing the pupil voice. She feels the council acts as the steering group for all the other school committees, and sees her own role as purely an advisory one.

This particular case study illustrates a number of important issues:

- Although the council members are involved in discussing the 'charmed circle' of common topics outlined by Baginsky and Hannam (1999: iii), they also talk about wider issues relating to social values. For instance, the pupils have been heavily involved in working with people in their local community and have established a statement of values that now underpin the school code of conduct.
- The pupils are clearly becoming creative and enterprising in both a business and social sense. They are engaged in a problem solving approach to tackling local community and social issues, and are also involved in handling school finances and ordering new school resources.
- The pupils participate in democratic forms of council elections, and all ages are represented.
- The teacher-leader takes a purely facilitative, advisory role.

- The commitment of teachers varies; while some organise class meetings regularly, others are less focused on this aspect of the councillors' work.

- Pupils liaise with a range of other pupil committees and this enhances the success of the democratic ethos: all pupils have the opportunity to participate in decision making at some point and the pupil council acts as the steering committee for the other pupil forums.

- Both councillors and non-councillors seem motivated and encouraged by the work of the pupil council. Pupils around the school feel that the council generally gives them opportunities to have a say in school decisions and enables them to help other members of the school community.

Other schools in the sample encouraged pupil members to create new school rules, to find solutions to bullying and to provide feedback about adult supervision in the playground. One group of councillors was involved in bidding for money from the Playground Improvement Group, which was comprised of teaching staff, the school's Family Learning Worker, members of the local community, parents and the headteacher. The children used this money to buy new resources for the playground. Teacher-leaders in all of the schools felt it was important for pupils to become involved in risk taking and business-related skills, such as handling finances and managing budgets. They were keen to promote pupil rights, confidence and self-esteem and to highlight pupils' collective social responsibilities.

Democratic practice varied in different schools; in some cases members were elected as a result of individual class votes and P7 pupils consulted with infant classes but younger children were not directly represented on councils. In other cases all class stages were represented. Meeting times also varied; while fortnightly meetings were in evidence in the above case study, other councils met only monthly or bi-monthly. In one school the teacher-leader tended to dominate discussions and to guide pupils in making pre-determined decisions. Although still participative in nature, this style of leadership was clearly less democratic. It represented what Hart

(1997: 41) describes as a 'consulted but informed' model as opposed to the 'child initiated and directed' model observed in the above case study.

In several schools, teacher-leaders were frustrated because their colleagues seemed reluctant to encourage councillors to feed back decisions to classmates following council meetings. In some schools, the pupil council appeared to be a more isolated vehicle for pupil consultation, since no other committees had been established. Although the pupils in the above case study seemed positive about the work of the council, a different view emerged in one of the schools: councillors had a higher regard for the value of the council than did non-council members. In this particular school many pupils were frustrated about not having their ideas listened to or taken seriously.

The pupils involved in the above case study seemed enthusiastic about creating ideas for social and community improvement. Their participation was guided by an ethos of promoting the pupil voice, celebrating the multicultural diversity in the local area and establishing shared community values. Pupil consultation in other schools was encouraging, if a little variable. Some schools seemed to create an agenda for change driven by pupil voices, where children and adults felt comfortable working in partnership. Others were still working towards this model. Where the pupil council acted at the centre of school-wide democratic practice, pupils appeared to bring wider issues to meetings. In other situations, agendas gravitated towards more basic, low level discussion and were driven by pupil criticism rather than activism.

Teacher-leaders in these primary schools recognised the contribution that the pupil councils played in developing aspects of citizenship and enterprise among pupils. They encouraged social, collectivist values and individualistic values. Indeed, these seemingly opposing agendas were often reconciled comfortably and pupils seemed to recognise the worth of what they were learning in terms of their own personal goals and the needs of others.

Case studies of practice in secondary schools

The positive examples emerging from case study primary schools, albeit with certain flaws and challenges, invite consideration of whether this democratic process could continue after pupils make the transition to secondary school. Maitles (2005) highlights the difference between upper primary and lower secondary schools in terms of the level of seriousness with which the councils are held:

> Pupils seem to have lots of rights and responsibilities in Primary 7 and fewer responsibilities and virtually no rights in Secondary 1. (Maitles, 2005: 31).

Other research suggests that pupils in early secondary school are marginalised in the decision making process (Denholm, 2006) and that pupils who have taken on important responsibilities at primary school are unlikely to encounter them again until the senior stages of secondary school (HMIE, 2006). Between 2004 and 2005, pupil council meetings were observed in the secondary schools to which the sample pupils had migrated. The case study in box 5.2 illustrates the marginalisation that can arise in the early secondary years. The case study school was linked to one of the feeder primary schools referred to above and pupils in S1 had come from a background of consultation and participation, albeit with some flaws in the democratic process. The evidence of practice raises issues about the transition from P7 to S1, its effect on the democratic process and the links created and sustained between aspects of citizenship and enterprise education.

Box 5.2: Case study of a secondary school pupil council

The S1-3 pupil council in this large secondary school, located within a fairly affluent socio-economic background, has been in place for five years. The council meets approximately six times per year when representatives from Secondary 1 to Secondary 3 get together with the Principal Teacher to discuss school improvement, organise charity events and visits to feeder primary schools. Council members ask for ideas and suggestions from the wider school in registration classes and this forms the basis of the council's agenda. At one meeting items raised by S1 and S2 pupils include

---

concerns about the lack of salt or tomato ketchup in the school canteen, the ongoing debate about school dress code and issues about inappropriate behaviour in the school corridors. There is also some feedback from S3 pupil members who recently visited some local primary schools. These councillors have brought back ideas from P7 pupils about extra-curricular activities they would like to be made available in school when they arrive next year. Three other S3 members provide feedback from a conference they attended on enterprise education, citing examples of projects that the school could become involved in.

The teacher-leader acts as chairperson of the committee, inviting members of sub-committees to give reports and pupils to give feed-back to new suggestions. He also makes some suggestions for new school resources and asks for council members' opinions. The pupils are able to speak at any time, but discussion is directed by the teacher-leader. At the end of the meeting, the teacher-leader invites two members of the pupil council to take over from him as chairperson, sharing this duty equally between them. Council members from S3 are asked to visit a local primary school to examine some new school resources, to send out letters to primary schools to invite P7 pupils to come in for a visit and to continue to monitor the feedback from pupils about the school canteen.

Among the changes that have come about as a result of the council's work pupils highlight the ongoing fundraising events that have raised money for local and international charities and the way in which the councillors have worked to improve the toilet facilities around the school. Although reasonably committed to the idea of the pupil council, some teachers in the school voted for meetings to take place at lunchtime or after school and not during classes. Pupil representatives from each registration class from each year are appointed to the pupil council on a voluntary basis, although if more than one volunteer per class comes forward then a voting process takes place. Pupils who are on the council feel that it provides them with an opportunity to have a say in how the school is run and feel privileged in being able to help the school become a better place. Older pupils particularly enjoy being able to visit other schools in order to reassure primary pupils about making the transition to secondary school and being able to talk on an equal level with the Principal Teacher. They feel that the pupils in the wider school look up to them and are encouraged by the work of the council. However non-councillors, particularly those in S1, have a different view. They feel generally unaware of the nature of the pupil council's work, or the decisions that are being made. Whereas in primary school the pupils were used to having an 'ideas box' where they could influence the pupil council agenda, they now no longer have that opportunity. Pupils feel that the councillors don't tell them anything and that they have very little influence around the school.

The case study illustrates that the senior pupils in the council are involved in quite challenging work, such as visiting feeder primary schools to strengthen primary/secondary liaison and attending educational conferences. However, younger pupils have no such opportunities and are confined to discussing issues relating to school dinners, uniforms and pupil behaviour. The teacher-leader takes a lead role in discussions and directs pupil decision making although there are plans for pupils to take over the chairing of some meetings.

By its very nature the case study illustrates that secondary schools differ from primary schools in terms of pupil representation. This is clearly an S1-3 council, with S4-6 pupils having their own forum. Within this sub-group more divisions seem to occur: it is clear that the S3 pupils take the lead and younger pupils are encouraged to be less vocal. Meetings are less frequent than they are in most primary schools, occurring only six times a year.

In other secondary schools pupils were rarely involved in handling school finances or in developing individual creativity or ambition. In one case, pupils organised a white band day to promote the *Make Poverty History* campaign and arranged for donations to be sent to Malawi. However, it was less common for pupils to liaise with other pupil committees, to organise financial bids or gain access to school budgets than it was in primary schools. Junior and senior pupils rarely worked together but tended to have separate pupil councils.

As in the primary schools, the commitment of teachers varied; while some were supportive, others were reluctant to let members out of class. In one secondary school in the sample teachers were enthusiastic about the council's work until the members began to initiate an anti-smoking lobby which applied to the school staff room. This reluctance to embrace the more inconvenient aspects of the councillors' ideas for activism reflects a tokenistic model; in Crick and Porter 's (1978: 7) words, '...if we want citizens we have to tolerate some of the unpredictable inconveniences of action and participation'. These secondary teachers clearly did not embrace this.

As in the above case study, pupils often had an inflated view of their ability to enact change in the school and this view was not shared by wider school populations. Many non-councillors seemed unaware of what the councillors were doing, and unimpressed by the lack of say they had in the council's decision making processes. Several comments by S1 pupils illustrate this well:

> Everything is decided for us here. *Emma, S1 pupil*

> In primary ... we used to have assembly every week and we got told about the pupil council ... but here we don't get told. *Scott, S1 pupil*

> They don't tell us anything ... nothing is happening that I am aware of ...they haven't changed anything. *Zaahir, S1 pupil*

> Not much has happened so far ... I haven't really seen them doing anything. *Amy, S1 pupil*

One teacher-leader thought that because the council had not organised prestigious or glamorous events recently other pupils may have been unaware of its work. However, perhaps the real reason was that teachers were unwilling to promote the pupil council during class contact time or to allocate time for post-council feedback. Two teacher-leaders summarised this clearly:

> If the pupils look at issues that don't affect staff, they're quite happy and benevolent ... I think a few people feel that the youngsters have more access to the senior management team than they do. *Classroom Teacher*

> (There is) too much focus on getting through exams and testing ... teachers concerned about getting through the workload (and) opposed to change. *Principal Teacher*

81

The hierarchy in these schools was powerful and the schools were seen as 'top-down authoritarian places' (Davies and Evans, 2002: 74). Also the culture of league tables and target-setting clearly detracted from the expression of authentic models of school democracy.

Summary

This chapter has explored the current expectation for schools to create a democratic framework for learning which enables pupil participation and promotes communitarian values arising from enterprise and citizenship education. The pupil council has been identified as a vehicle for democratic participation in schools but its potential for challenging the school hierarchy and for enabling pupil learning in enterprise and citizenship education has been questioned.

The Scottish case studies outlined in this chapter provide us with a useful point of reference and help us to understand the positive and negative aspects of these councils in promoting such learning. The main findings are summarised as follows:

- Many Scottish primary school pupil councils appear to give pupils a genuine opportunity to have a voice and to promote communitarian principles that relate to both enterprise and citizenship education. Where councils work alongside a range of other pupil committees and act at the centre of school-wide participative practice, the focus on democracy is clearly at its highest (Baginsky and Hannam, 1999).

- However, many councillors have a higher regard than non-council members for the value of the council. This is more of an issue in secondary schools.

- The main sources of inconsistency in translating enterprise and citizenship policy into practice via pupil councils can be identified as the continued existence of school authoritarianism and the pressures associated with the attainment agenda and prescriptive curriculum guidelines.

■ Pupil marginalisation, inconsistent models of representation, teacher resistance and tokenistic models of consultation can stifle the expression of a reconciled model of creativity, enterprise and civic engagement through pupil councils. These issues are found more commonly in secondary schools.

Even where the practice in pupil councils is encouraging, it is important that the democratic ethos is upheld through pupils' other experiences of school life. These other educational experiences are examined in chapter 6.

Pause for reflection

Even where genuine forums for consultation exist in a school it is important to monitor their effectiveness and to update their practice accordingly. In this way teachers can avoid tokenistic practice or pupil apathy. If you have recently been involved in setting up a pupil council, it is useful to establish how the pupil councillors feel about the work of the council and how effective the wider school perceives the new council to be. If you are involved in coordinating a more established pupil council, it is useful to monitor the success of the council over a longer period of time and to use this information as the basis for making changes to current practice. The questions below enable you to explore what council members regard as their main priorities, how motivated they are and how successful they perceive the council's work to be. The questions for non-councillors will allow you to establish how the wider school views the functions of the council and the extent to which the members are achieving their goals. Student teachers and academics who are interested in studying pupil councils in more depth will find the observation schedule helpful. Using the observations as the basis for further discussion with teacher-leaders will enable you to make a judgement about the democratic framework in place that supports the pupil voice.

Discussion questions: council members:

■ What do you think the main aims of the pupil council are?

■ How do you feel about being on the council?

- Which parts are enjoyable/not so enjoyable?
- Why did you want to be a member of the pupil council?
- What are your friends' views about the pupil council?
- What practical changes have come about as a result of your work on the pupil council?

Discussion questions: non-council members

- What do you think the role of a council member is?
- What do you think of the work of the pupil council?
- Do you think that appropriate people have been elected?
- Do you feel involved in creating ideas for the pupil council?
- Did you want to stand for the pupil council? Why/why not?
- What do you think the role of the teacher-leader is?

Pupil Council Observation Schedule:

School:	No of students present:
Date of meeting:	Year groups represented:
Staff present:	Location:
Time:	Duration:

Items discussed:

Level of interaction/involvement

Conduct of meeting

Follow-up/decisions reached:

Additional notes:

6

Moving beyond the pupil council: whole-school community projects and controversial issues

The pupil council has been identified as one means of enabling pupils to learn the skills and qualities necessary for active, responsible citizenship and ethical enterprise. However, chapter 1 also identified the need for pupil consultation and participation to permeate the whole school and for pupils to engage in discussion and learning about matters of particular interest to them as part of the school curriculum. Indeed, Covell and Howe (2001) outline the danger of having isolated pockets of pupil consultation:

> If adolescents learn that they have rights but experience these rights only when with a particular teacher, perceived hypocrisy may replace perceived support. (Covell and Howe, 2001: 40)

Democratic participation, as a pre-requisite for the full expression of education for citizenship and enterprise, needs to be extended beyond the confines of the isolated pupil council or the individual classroom. This involves creating a participatory and democratic culture throughout the whole school, which includes the opportunity for pupils to discuss controversial issues of their own choice. This chapter examines the practice within two of the sample primary schools described earlier and illustrates positive examples of whole school and classroom-based approaches to democratic engagement. Case studies and illustrative examples illuminate the way in which democratic school practice can lead to enhanced levels of community welfare, social tolerance and political literacy.

Creating responsible, tolerant citizens

One of the sample schools was located in a small port town on the west coast of Scotland, set against the backdrop of severe social deprivation. Challenges in the local area included high crime, drug abuse and unemployment rates. The school had suffered in the past from violent reactions from pupils and their parents and there was a continuing problem with vandalism. A new headteacher had been appointed in 2001 and had created a new vision: she regarded the school as a central and focal point within the community. She strove to get pupils more involved in making decisions about their learning, to get parents involved in their children's education and to instil a sense of responsibility among pupils and their families for the welfare of their own community.

The school had a very active pupil council, and councillors liaised with other pupil committees in the school such as the playground improvement group. Pupil members discussed many school policy issues and had access to school finances. The relationship between the children and staff had become much more open and pupils were now regarded as fully participative members in the decision making process.

The headteacher was committed to the idea of school democratisation and saw enterprise as the starting point for this. She viewed enterprise education as a process of active learning where children are encouraged to be innovative and creative within a range of contexts, including those contexts so often associated with citizenship education.

The case study in box 6.1 illustrates how pupil innovation was encouraged and how the children were consulted about their learning. It demonstrates that such innovation and consultation can have positive effects on the whole school community.

Box 6.1: Case study – a cross-cultural community arts project

At one meeting of the school's pupil council early in 2005 the head-teacher talks to the councillors about the possibility of doing a school community arts project. She has become aware of a cross-cultural project which involves schools and communities across Scotland investigating north west coast artefacts, exploring their own heritage and natural environment and creating uniquely Scottish totem poles. Brotus Rural Crafts, run by a Scottish Bodger and a group of First Nations carvers from Canada, work with groups of children for up to two weeks, running hands-on carving sessions with accompanying storytelling, drawing and music workshops. Through this collaboration the groups create new, contemporary art works that reflect the lives and interests of their own community. An official pole raising event marks the end of each project, accompanied by First Nations ceremonial song, dance and official regalia.

Pupil council members carry out some research into the project on the internet and are enthusiastic about its content. The headteacher introduces the pupil council to the Scottish Bodger and his team, who explain that pupils will create drawings related to stories about their local heritage and will erect a life-sized totem pole in their own school playground. The headteacher sees the potential for linking citizenship education with creativity and enterprise:

> It's about planning, problem solving, teamwork, using initiative, using their best skills and recognising skills other people bring. *Headteacher*

The P7 class become the lead partners in the venture but the pupils also ensure that the rest of the school is involved. A highlight of the project is the opportunity to engage in listening, talking and writing: local historians, retired teachers, artists, story tellers, musicians, grounds development people and a local farmer come in and share ancient tales about the local community with pupils. Children are thus introduced to aspects of their local heritage. In time, the headteacher notes a change in the way the children view their own community; she feels that they have developed a pride in their surroundings for the first time:

> If they had to write about their views of where they live (before) ... (they'd say) it was 'crap here', 'nothing to do', 'nowhere to go', 'nothing interesting'. They won't say that now. It's like, 'oh there's a ghost up in the cave', 'the guy got thrown off the Gallie Craig because he wouldn't give a recipe for heather whisky', 'if you go down to Kirkmadrine it's haunted on a Tuesday and Thursday night' and 'that's the first Christian stones up there in Scotland' ... and on and on it goes. *Headteacher*

The intensity of learning about their own local heritage is combined with learning about the culture and heritage of the Canadian First Nations people. Pupils feel proud that they are the first pupils in the school's history to have done such a project. They feel that they have learned a lot about their own culture and the culture of the Canadians:

> It's given us an idea of what people in Canada do ... and what their culture's like ... and what this town was like in the olden days through the stories we've heard. *Craig, P7 boy*

The project provides many opportunities for active, pupil-centred learning, such as involving children in creating updates on the progress with the totem pole for the school website. Pupils describe the decisions they make about the design of the pole, the groups they work in and the publicity work they carry out:

> We had twelve pictures and we had to decide which was going at the top (of the pole), which was going in the middle ... the bottom ... how high it was going to be ... where the totem pole would be placed. *Amanda, P7 girl*

> (We decide) what groups we're going to be in ... we have press groups, because they were doing the press releases and some people would do images for the stories. We had people that would go and find out things about totem poles. *Jack, P7 boy*

The P7 class teacher is enthusiastic about the children's new insight into the local and global community. She values the opportunity the pupils have had for research into Canadian First Nations and the history of their own local community. She feels that pupils have gained more confidence and developed a heightened sense of intellectual curiosity:

> It has given them inspiration to go and visit places in the local area and meet the folks with the knowledge ... It has inspired them to ask

questions about things ... given them a bit of confidence that, if they do meet someone in the future, they'll know how to go about asking questions ... They were listening, talking, writing ... they were also reading things, searching the internet. I would say it's boosted my class's language skills 100%. *Class Teacher*

The whole school is involved in creating the pictures, working with the First Nations and listening to the local story tellers. The project is therefore very holistic in nature: children at different stages of the school talk about their interest in it and are motivated by seeing an end product in sight. They praise the work of the pupil council for initiating the project, as well as many other practical changes that have enhanced their experience of school life:

(The pupil council) is extremely successful because you get listened to and there have been a lot of changes ... And we've got so many things outside now that we can never be bored. *Kimberley, P4 girl*

The P7 class teacher struggles to see the links with enterprise education since she sees enterprise as being primarily about business, However, the headteacher takes a different view. She believes that the project has addressed many elements of enterprise as well as citizenship education:

(Children have learned about) race and language because 'Native American Indian' is not the phrase that these guys want us to use, it's definitely 'Canadian First Nation'. They understand that the guys come from different nations, have different dialect. It's been about respect for different cultures ... The guys tell jokes against themselves using the word 'Indian' ... It's great for the kids to be able to see that's a term they use in fun but it is derogatory. *Headteacher*

The projects they are doing as a whole are really developing values and attitudes for enterprise ... it's important to talk about budgets, reality, feasibility ... I ask the pupil council members to take their ideas to the playground improvement group and sell them: they have to think about – why should they give you £4000? *Headteacher*

Drawing parents in to help with the community-based projects has been challenging because of their lack of confidence. However, the headteacher has noted an increased level of tolerance and respect for the local school environment because of the ownership the children now have:

When I came here four years ago we had twelve broken windows a week and the playground was a shit hole with dog dirt and needles and parents fighting in the playground hitting other people's children ...it was a war zone ... now we [only] have the odd stone thrown ...The pupil council decided we should spend £4,000 on the adventure playground, £2,000 on toys, £2,000 on game zones, now £4,000 on the totem pole ... Every year we go to the pupil council and say 'what do you want?' and then we do the budget and then we do the project ... it's down to ownership. *Headteacher*

This case study illustrates the participatory ethos that had been established over several years in this school and how the pupil council was now at the centre of school-wide democratic practice. The headteacher and staff consulted with the council members on aspects related to playground improvement, budgeting and issues related to learning and teaching. The cross-cultural community arts project, initiated by the pupil council, enabled pupils in P7 to take the lead in exploring aspects of their own heritage as well as learning to respect and celebrate cultural diversity. Pupils across different stages of the school also participated in the ceremonial artwork, dance and music associated with the Canadian First Nation carvers. Many of them were also involved in planning the project. Pupils were engaged in problem solving, teamwork, negotiation and compromise.

The local visitors developed children's interest in their own heritage while the Canadians made them aware of cultural diversity and the dangers associated with discriminatory racial language. The children became more confident, more able to ask questions and to recognise the value of their own local surroundings. A sense of ownership emerged from the work of the pupil council, its associated committees and the individual classes in the school. This led to a decrease in the level of vandalism within the local area.

Education for citizenship is about creating a sense of belonging, the opportunity to exercise both rights and responsibilities and the ability to communicate opinions and participate in decision making (Osler, 2005). Pupils feel more valued and engaged if they are consulted about school projects and asked to plan the projects themselves. If the children are also encouraged to interact with both the local and global community, they will develop social tolerance and learn to respect human rights and cultural diversity. As Starkey (2005) argues, language education provides an opportunity for pupils to develop respect for civilisations which are different from their own. Pupils gain the opportunity to talk and listen to people from other cultures and to build personal friendships and relationships. In the case study above language education was supporting the implementation of education for citizenship: pupils listened to local historical stories, wrote reports about their heritage and created images for the totem pole. They also talked about controversial issues such as racism and discrimination.

The headteacher felt that a holistic approach to enterprise education was at the core of the whole project. Pupils were learning to bid for funds from various school sources, to take risks and to engage in critical thinking skills. Elements of enterprise and citizenship were dovetailed, which resulted in both agendas becoming redefined. While enterprise was viewed in relation to local and global community welfare, citizenship opportunities also enabled pupils to become involved in budgeting and risk taking. However, some teachers had not yet fully embraced the broader notion of enterprise and defined the project solely in terms of citizenship.

This cross-cultural project was underpinned by a maximal approach towards enterprise and citizenship education and the creation of a democratic school ethos. Pupils' engagement in this project and others like it led to the school playground and surrounding area becoming transformed from what was described as a war zone. Pupils and their families became more responsible in their interactions with the local community and more tolerant of other cultures. This supports Harber's (2004: 137) view that learning democratic skills and values through institutional and curriculum organisation can minimise internal violence. In such cases a consultative ethos replaces violent and destructive tendencies with 'a proclivity to reason, open-mindedness and fairness and the practice of cooperation, bargaining, compromise and accommodation.' The evidence from this case study endorses this view.

Enhancing Political Literacy

One other school in the sample was set within an industrial, working-class town with a fairly mixed socio-economic background. P7 pupils (aged 11) were regularly encouraged by their class teacher to bring in news stories that were of interest to them as part of a weekly International News Day session. These sessions enabled pupils to talk about social and political interests and they often demonstrated mature views and opinions. Pupils were granted total freedom of expression by the teacher, although they had to justify their opinions. The research on primary pupils' understanding of enterprise showed that these pupils often referred to political figures such as Tony Blair and George Bush. At the time of the outbreak of the Iraq war in March 2003 some pupils were definite in their views about Bush:

> President Bush ... there's some ways he's enterprising and some ways he's stupid as well. He has to talk in front of millions and millions of people in his country ... but I don't think he should go to war with Iraq ... he's power crazy. *Taylor, P7 pupil*

My initial discussions with the pupils led to a subsidiary case study that spanned a period of one year (Maitles and Deuchar, 2004; 2004a). Box 6.2 illustrates the way in which the P7 teacher's methodology was having an impact on the pupils' political literacy. It also illustrates the way in which their political literacy subsequently evolved as a result of their P7 classroom experiences.

Box 6.2: Case study – bringing controversial issues into the classroom

The P7 class teacher in this school views enterprise education in a holistic sense and feels that an enterprising teacher creates an ethos where pupils are free to express their opinions. She encourages pupils to discuss many controversial issues. The issues for which she has noted particular pupil interest in recent years included teenage pregnancy, the use and misuse of drugs, animal rights and the debate about the teaching of religion in schools. This year she has noticed that pupils have become interested in terrorism and issues surrounding the Iraq war.

This teacher encourages pupils to express their opinions and sees the importance of demonstrating the value of these opinions to children. She also shares many of her own views openly in class. She challenges pupils' views and encourages them to challenge her own opinions. Although proven to be highly successful, the teacher feels that this approach is not as common among other teachers as it should be. She thinks that many of her colleagues are reluctant to encourage pupils to express their opinions because they fear losing control of classroom discipline. She also thinks that teachers who have the confidence and courage to allow pupil participation can minimise indiscipline because children will be less frustrated at school.

In discussion groups P7 pupils debate the pros and cons of Britain and America invading Iraq in 2003. Some feel that the outbreak of war was inevitable because Saddam Hussein has bombs and is 'trying to do what Hitler was trying to do – rule the world.' Others think that Bush and Blair are to blame and are also dictators. Some pupils are passionate about key events during the war, such as the day they saw the Iraqi people celebrate as they tore down Saddam Hussein's statue in Baghdad. Some pupils talk about their uneasiness with the celebrations; they feel concerned about the anarchy taking place and the need to rebuild Iraqi towns and cities. Other pupils focus their attention on the cruelty of the Saddam regime and are more encouraged by the celebrations that followed the fall of that regime. The pupils' opinions about the future of Iraq are enlightening: most focus their attention on the need to continue the search for Saddam Hussein but more reflective pupils see the need to introduce a new democratic form of government.

One year later the pupils continue to hold strong opinions about the Iraq war following their transition to secondary school in 2004. Indeed, these opinions have become even stronger and their views about Bush and Blair have become more negative. The pupils are concerned that the leaders do not listen to the public and that they went ahead with the war in spite of the general mood of the country. They view the war with even more distaste than before, as the following comment illustrates:

> It was a waste of time, because they haven't found anything. They said there were bombs there and that's why they went in the first

place. But they've not found anything so it's been a total waste of time. *James, S1 pupil*

The pupils also reflect upon the capture of Saddam Hussein. Far from seeing this as a solution, they think that the situation in Iraq has worsened. They also see a link between events in Iraq and the more recent atrocity in Madrid. Their views about the continued threat of terrorism and their fears for the future are bleak:

It's going to be harder for us in the future. The world's just rotting away, with all these bombings ... There's probably enough bombs to just blow up the world whenever anyone wants it. *Craig, S1 pupil*

Finally, although the pupils were fairly apathetic about the idea of peace protests at the beginning of the war, they now seem more supportive of the idea. But they are also convinced that the protesters' words will fall on deaf ears. One pupil's comment illustrates this clearly:

They're speaking their word and I think they've got a point ... but no one's going to bother listening to them. *Steven, S1 pupil*

The pupils clearly have a great deal of interest in this issue and are determined to try and understand the full implications of current international events. They are concerned about social justice and committed towards enacting social change. Although they appear to have become increasingly more cynical towards the motives of political leaders, they also demonstrate an increasing passion for discussing and debating political and social issues.

The pupils in the above case study had clearly been influenced by their P7 teacher's open approach towards discussion and debate. This teacher had conceptualised the meaning of enterprise in school around her particular style of teaching, rather than associating it with any particular form of project *per se*. Her model of teaching was built around developing a respectful, trusting relationship with the pupils and encouraging them to develop their opinions about highly controversial social and political issues.

The P7 pupils displayed evidence of their emerging knowledge and understanding, skills, aptitudes and values, all of which relate well to the current citizenship education agenda. They had good knowledge of topical and contemporary issues at international levels, as well as an awareness of the nature of democracy and the way in which the future of Iraq could and should be decided. They showed growing understanding of the nature of diversity and social conflict and a concern for the common good. In addition, their reflective comments about the underlying causes of the war illustrated that they took a critical approach to the evidence presented via the mass media. These pupils had a strong concern for human dignity, equality and the need to resolve conflict diplomatically. They were able to recognise forms of manipulation being used by political leaders in their attempts to justify the need for war. The pupils were creative and enterprising in their capacity to imagine alternative realities and futures for the people of Iraq (QCA, 1998; LTScotland, 2002).

The class teacher's approach was the key to all of this learning. This teacher clearly took up the stance of critical affirmation advocated by Ashton and Watson (1998) in allowing pupils to develop their arguments. She viewed enterprising teaching as a means of creating a participatory classroom ethos and a vehicle for enhancing pupils' political literacy. The relationship, trust and respect between pupils and teacher was central to her approach and the discussion of highly controversial issues provided an essential context for enterprise and citizenship to unite and engage pupils in learning.

Summary
This chapter has argued that for pupils to experience citizenship and enterprise education in its fullest sense they need to be exposed to a democratic culture that extends beyond the confines of the pupil council into the classroom and the rest of the school. The two case studies presented in this chapter provide illustrations of the way in which two schools managed to do this. The main conclusions of these case studies are:

- Consulting pupils about the projects they study enhances their motivation through giving them ownership and making them feel more valued. Pupil councils can play a valuable role in initiating such projects and ensuring that pupils at all stages of the school are involved.

■ Cross-cultural projects which involve pupils interacting with the local and global community can lead to increased tolerance, responsibility and respect. Pupils will begin to value their own community and will also gain more respect for cultural diversity. Such projects are most effective if they are underpinned by a combined and broad focus on enterprise and citizenship, where individualistic and collectivist values meet.

■ When a respectful, trusting relationship between teacher and pupils exists and the teacher encourages the pupils to develop their opinions, even the most controversial issues can be sensitively discussed in classrooms. When teachers adopt a broad view of enterprise and associate it with a participatory style of discussing such issues, this can have a profound and lasting impact on pupils' developing political literacy.

■ However, there are still some barriers to initiating a broad focus on enterprise and citizenship, which is underpinned by a democratic ethos: some teachers view enterprise education in a narrow sense and cannot make the links with citizenship and others are afraid to adopt a participative approach to classroom organisation for fear of losing control of discipline. This confirms earlier views about the continued dominance of authoritarian and didactic models of teaching across the world (Harber, 1995; Forrester, 2003; Harber, 2004).

Pause for reflection

The case studies have illustrated the need to create a democratic culture in schools, which will enable pupils to initiate projects and discussion topics of interest to them. It is useful to define the concepts that you associate with democracy, as a starting point for assessing the extent to which school projects and teaching approaches are guided by these concepts. The exercise on page 99, adapted from a previous activity by Claire (2004), allows you to identify your own priorities for democracy. You can use these to evaluate the way in which particular projects are implemented: do pupils have the opportunity for freedom of speech? Are there opportunities for pupils to display tolerance and respect, to vote on particularly controversial issues? Any serious gaps in provision will need to be addressed before a school can truly regard itself as democratic. Teachers and student teachers can also use this exercise as the basis for engaging in a self-assessment activity to determine how democratic their teaching styles are.

Use the statements about democracy found below and do a diamond ranking exercise with colleagues: decide which is the most important idea for democracy, which are the next two most important ideas, then the next three, then two again, finally ending up with the one which you think is least important. You may find it useful to substitute your own ideas for some of the statements given here. Whatever ideas you choose to prioritise, can you identify the extent to which current projects and teaching approaches in your school are underpinned by these concepts? Where are the gaps?

Tolerance and respect for others	A forum to express opinions about current, controversial issues	Everyone has the right and opportunity to vote
Willingness to allow others their point of view	Principles of being fair to the minority	The majority decides
Opportunities for enacting change in the community	Regular elections so that voters can change the group in power	Freedom of speech

(Concepts adapted from Claire, 2004: 12)

7

Future directions for citizenship, enterprise and learning

The world today is characterised by seemingly paradoxical values. On the one hand there is an increased focus on democracy and human rights. On the other there is a growing culture of fear, mistrust and a propensity to demonise young people. The need for strengthening community values, social tolerance and responsibility is combined with a worldwide focus on growing prosperous and competitive global economies. In many parts of the world the focus on third way politics has driven this dual agenda forward. But teachers struggle to combine the market led agenda with their own values: pressures associated with exams and target setting and with preparing pupils to contribute toward economic strength detract from achieving the things that brought them into the profession. In many ways education for citizenship represents what many primary teachers have always wanted: the chance to prepare pupils for life through personal, social and moral development. The new broader focus on enterprise is seen as being part of that process: encouraging creativity and innovation within social and ethical contexts.

Part I of this book argued that, in spite of this, neo-liberal values continue to influence educational practice in many parts of the world. Enterprise education is often still associated with business-related themes and economic fundamentalism. In addition, despite the acknowledged need for democratic values to guide the organisation of schools, international evidence suggests that schooling is an essentially authoritarian experience for many pupils (Harber, 2004). In Britain New Labour policy has been described by some as a 'bastard Thatcherism', with the rhetoric of social justice and equity serving only to mask the continuation of neo-liberal agendas (Lawton, 2005).

Part II turned the spotlight on Scotland, where key educational policies and guidelines suggest a communitarian model for enterprise and citizenship education. The interview and case study evidence presented here suggests that many Scottish teachers and pupils are moving towards a model of social entrepreneurship, guided by communitarian principles. The primary schools examined often brought enterprise and citizenship together under one umbrella and thus redefined both agendas. Enterprise education was focused on a more holistic model of active learning, participation and social innovation. Citizenship education encompassed community involvement, political literacy and values but also enabled the expression of individualism and business-related skills.

But still looming among this good practice is the threat of the neo-liberal and neo-capitalist agendas. Those initiating good practice faced authoritarian views from their colleagues. A minority of teachers continued to define enterprise education in its narrowest sense and to implement projects solely based on business and money making themes. These influences meant that a minority of pupils continued to associate enterprise with purely individualistic themes, although most interpreted it more broadly. The pressure of bureaucratic control, accountability and imposed goals sometimes stifled teachers' vision for holistic models of enterprise and citizenship. Even where primary schools provided real success stories, the positive impact on pupils' learning was quickly undermined in early secondary school where a minimal, tokenistic model often prevailed.

So, along with identifying pockets of good practice, this book shows what prevents this practice becoming more widespread. So what of the future? A school should represent a 'micro-social or political community' (Oliver and Heater, 1994: 157). But what hope is there that the influence of the neo-liberal agenda will subside, enabling schools to represent communitarian values? And will curriculum reform enable teachers to be freed from the stranglehold of the attainment agenda? This final chapter, considers the direction in which education in Britain is going and the extent to which this may enable the full expression of enterprise and citizenship.

Political focus on respect and discipline

The technicalist, managerial approach adopted by New Labour is set to continue (Lawton, 2005). The *Respect Action Plan* of January 2006 points to the need for civility, good manners, acting unselfishly and helping others (Respect Task Force, 2006). It specifically mentions the role of schools in promoting the values and behaviour that support respect, and highlights the need to promote good discipline as a means of increasing teacher and pupil morale. This is confirmed in the recent schools white paper *Higher Standards, Better Schools for All* (DfES, 2005) and the *Education and Inspections Bill 2006* (DfES, 2006), where behaviour is highlighted as a major concern for school staff:

> The Bill ... will create, for the first time, a clear statutory right for school staff to discipline pupils – putting an end to the 'You can't tell me what to do' culture. (DfES, 2006: 2)

The bill makes tackling bad behaviour a priority and suggests that teachers need new powers to discipline students for 'not following instructions'. It emphasises the need for schools to have greater scope for implementing pupil detention and for 'confiscating inappropriate items'. Parents of suspended and excluded pupils should receive prosecution notices when their children are found in public places during school hours. And the bill makes 'reintegration interviews' compulsory for pupils who have been excluded from school for some time (DfES, 2006: 8-9).

These new regulations are hardly democratic. Describing a culture of 'you can't tell me what to do' and creating a counter-attack is clearly authoritarian. Such rhetoric denies young people's democratic right of freedom of expression and of free dissent. The bill suggests that pupils have to follow teachers' instructions or face the prospect of punishment or exclusion. Words such as 'instructions', 'force', 'detention', 'confiscation', 'exclusion', 'prosecution' and 're-integration' all have the effect of demonising youth. They certainly do not fit a democratic, participative model that encourages social criticism and activism. In Lawton's words (2005: 164): 'Many schools ... manage to alienate their students by the authoritarian atmosphere in the school and very poor teacher-pupil relations.'

The Discipline Task Group's *Better Behaviour – Better Learning* report (Scottish Executive, 2001a) gives advice about behavioural issues in Scottish schools. It recommends that positive behaviour should be promoted through encouraging pupil decision making and by establishing pupil buddying and mentoring schemes. In 2004 the Scottish Executive reports that 91 per cent of primary schools pupils and 73 per cent of secondary pupils feel that they are involved in school decision-making processes. However, only a third of the 11 year olds surveyed say that they like school a lot, and by age 13 this has dropped to around a quarter (Scottish Executive, 2004).

The Scottish focus on active participation linked to promoting positive behaviour promotes the citizenship agenda. Yet although many pupils feel involved in decision making, they are still not motivated by school. The evidence in this book gives us some explanations: in the schools surveyed it appeared that pupil participation was only invited in some classrooms, while others remained authoritarian. So, even if pupils feel they make decisions in some contexts, they may also experience autocratic models of teaching and school management.

Political perspectives on school organisation and curriculum content must change before a truly democratic model can emerge. But it is predicted that if Gordon Brown succeeds Tony Blair in office, his premiership is unlikely to mean any let up in the drive towards the respect agenda or the target driven push for higher standards, greater efficiency, business involvement and job-related skills (Baker, 2006).

The national curriculum in England: promoting a maximal model?

The citizenship attainment targets and links to enterprise within the English national curriculum indicate the extent to which a maximal model is likely to prevail. At key stages 1 and 2 pupils are expected to learn about themselves as developing and changing individuals and as members of their communities (National Curriculum Online, 2006). They are to be presented with opportunities and made aware of their responsibilities for themselves, for others and for the environment. Later, pupils learn about the wider world and the interdependence of communities within it, and this is linked to the need for developing a sense of moral responsibility. Key stage 1 pupils will learn to resolve arguments and take an active part in their school and its neighbourhood, while key stage 2 pupils will learn to take part more fully in school and community activities as well as relating their own choices to their effect on 'local, national or global issues' (National Curriculum Online, 2006).

At key stage 2 pupils are expected to 'develop confidence and responsibility and make the most of their abilities' (National Curriculum Online, 2006), so should be encouraged to talk and write about their opinions on topical issues. They should be taught to think positively about themselves, to make responsible choices and to take action. They should also develop an understanding of the contribution they can make to society through work roles and learn how to manage money. Pupils should be prepared to play an active role as citizens through researching topical issues, becoming aware of social responsibilities and resolving conflict. Pupils should learn what democracy means and recognise the range of Britain's national and ethnic identities and the way in which economic choices affect individuals and communities.

Enterprise themes are prominent in certain key stage 2 programmes. In *Our Community* pupils look at different jobs and roles within the community and learn about the importance of decision making, voting, paying taxes and working together (Young Enterprise, 2006). In *Our City* pupils learn about the construction industry and the dependency that exists between workers and services. And in *Our World* they learn about global interdependence and how rich countries should strive to balance economic development with the need for ethical and responsible behaviour towards poorer countries.

Individual rights, confidence and opportunity are combined with social responsibility in the curriculum. Pupils are expected to explore issues of personal concern and to become aware of their potential to take action both in and outside school. Equality and diversity is featured and pupils combine their knowledge of economic wealth creation with ethical and moral considerations. A flexible framework of specific learning outcomes is more conducive to encouraging pupil participation than are detailed programmes of study.

However, research indicates that schools actually transferring these principles into practice is another matter. Kerr (2004) reports on the initial findings of the Citizenship Education Longitudinal Study conducted by researchers at the National Foundation for Educational Research (NfER). The findings indicate that teacher-led approaches to citizenship-related topics predominate over participatory, active approaches in the classroom and that teachers are often hostile to and dismissive of citizenship education. This supports evidence presented in chapter 2 of this book that heavy reliance on textbooks suggests that citizenship education is taught conservatively in many English schools (Davies and Issitt, 2005). Maitles (2005) suggests that over-concentration on exam targets impacts negatively on the education for citizenship agenda and that the pressure on schools to achieve high GCSE grades in subjects like mathematics, language and science fosters rote learning and undemocratic models of teaching (Maitles, 2005).

While many schools may still be at an early stage of implementing the new initiatives associated with education for citizenship, a lip service approach looks likely to continue. The combination of the attainment agenda and a prescriptive national curriculum is likely to stifle the flexible, participatory learning outcomes suggested by the citizenship framework. Likewise the focus on enterprise education will still be seen in more narrow terms.

The Scottish *Curriculum for Excellence*

The Curriculum Review Group in Scotland (2004) has set out the Scottish Executive's vision for transforming Scottish education by 2007. *A Curriculum for Excellence* seeks to establish the values, purposes and principles of education in Scotland for children between the ages of 3 and 18. The review group urges the reconciliation of creativity and enterprise with thoughtful and responsible citizenship in their vision for 21st century education:

> Our aspiration is to enable all children to develop their capabilities as successful learners, confident individuals, responsible citizens and effective contributors to society. (Curriculum Review Group, 2004: 3)

If we examine the specific capacities it identifies, we see that developing successful learners acknowledges the need for instilling determination, creating new ideas and a propensity to think creatively and independently. The goal is to achieve confident individuals who have ambition, self respect, an ability to live independently and assess risk and make informed decisions. At the same time the review group highlights the need to develop pupils' capacity to become responsible citizens with a focus on respect, and for them to 'participate responsibly in political, economic, social and cultural life'. 'Informed, ethical views of complex issues' should be developed and pupils should become effective contributors, developing an 'enterprising attitude' which includes 'resilience', self-reliance and initiative.

This new vision for Scotland steers thinking on confident, active and thoughtful participation in a more pragmatic direction. *A Curriculum for Excellence* calls for a broad view of both citizenship and enterprise education. The recommendations are driven by a focus on communitarian ideals whereby individual interests are advanced through ethical community interaction. Independent creativity, ambition, initiative and participation rights should be developed in pupils, while tolerance, respect and ethical considerations are viewed as being equally important. Enterprising attitudes are seen in a holistic sense: pupils are to be encouraged to participate in economic contexts, but also to contribute towards social and cultural innovation. However, Smith (2006: 20) is among critics who find that the tone of the new proposals reflects a political statement about the continuation of the 'pressure to succeed, to be excellent, to raise standards'.

The Curriculum Review Group aims to de-clutter the primary curriculum and restructure early secondary education to enable more progression and continuity across transition. More space should be created for teachers to meet individual pupil interests and needs and to exercise judgements about how best to engage individual pupils. Policy and practice should be underpinned by democratic values, enabling pupils to commit to making active and ethical contributions to society. A single curriculum 3-18 should allow for an appropriate pace of learning at critical points, such as the move from primary to secondary education (Curriculum Review Group, 2004). National testing procedures are to be revised to introduce a national assessment bank and opportunities for pupils to have personal learning plans. Assessment is to be less prescriptive and take greater account of teachers' judgements. The Scottish *Assessment is for Learning* initiative seeks to have a streamlined and coherent system of assessment for Scottish schools that will support learning by 2007 (Scottish Executive, 2005).

Yet First Minister Jack McConnell has hinted at controversial new plans to introduce a new basic skills test as part of Labour's manifesto for the 2007 Holyrood elections. This follows on from reports from the corporate world suggesting that one in three businesses have to send staff for remedial catch-up lessons in basic literacy and numeracy (Fraser, 2006). Critics have argued that the creation of another new exam undermines the work of those involved in the curriculum review process and contradicts the current policy to reduce the assessment burden.

After 2007 it will be important to examine the impact of curriculum change on the following key areas:

- the way in which the reforms enable teachers to de-clutter the primary curriculum and create more space for pupils to engage in discussing controversial, social issues and make decisions about learning and teaching.

- the impact of change on S1/2, and the extent to which continuity and progression enables pupils to have as much, or more, responsibility in secondary school as they do in primary school.

- the extent to which the reforms reduce the burden of national assessment and attainment targets, enabling teachers to prioritise developing a maximal approach to citizenship and enterprise education

- the extent to which Scottish education enables pupils to become motivated, successful, confident learners and to become ethical, responsible and active in their contribution to society.

21st century education or 19th century schools?

In England the national curriculum provides teachers with a flexible approach towards addressing key learning outcomes for citizenship, with an emphasis on holistic views of enterprise. However, the prescriptive model that guides the implementation of the wider national curriculum combined with the continued focus on exams and league tables appears to stifle this agenda. This leads to the continued dominance of teacher-led approaches and rote learning. In addition, new legislation serves to widen the focus on firmer, punitive approaches towards pupil behaviour management. This agenda, which includes a strong focus on an authoritarian school model, will surely act as a deterrent to the full expression of enterprise and citizenship.

The new vision for a reformed curriculum model in Scotland offers hope. The values that underpin it appear to fit with a holistic model of enterprise education as well as the principles underpinning the need for active and responsible citizenship. We are assured that its full implementation will enable more space for pupil-led agendas, will enhance primary-secondary continuity and reduce the burden of a prescriptive attainment agenda. Thus the challenges identified in earlier chapters of this book might be addressed at last, as long as the focus on excellence and success are interpreted within the context of communitarian principles rather than neo-liberal ones and any plans for additional new national tests and exams are shelved.

Future research must explore the way in which teachers, pupils and schools are encouraged to interpret the framework and to reconcile individual creativity and enterprise with citizenship and democracy.

It is certainly desirable for schools to be 'wholly competitive and wholly civic-minded' (Davies *et al*, 2001: 261). This may indeed be possible if a broad perspective on enterprise and citizenship programmes is taken which upholds democratic and communitarian principles as shown in the diagram in the introduction to this book. However, the realisation of this vision will require a change of culture in schools. This book has shown that authoritarian approaches towards teaching and pupil management is preventing the expression of this broad agenda. Schools need to be models of democratic, pluralist and enterprising societies more than ever before, since their future may shape the future of the world:

> Schools at their best are idealised microcosms of society and the world. A significant challenge is to develop this model and see our schools as vehicles for conveying concepts of democracy and human rights to society at large. In this way we may attempt to make our communities and the wider world reflect more adequately the values and global perspectives that we already practice in our schools. (Osler and Starkey, 2002: 172)

The last words come from a group of P7 pupils in a Scottish school. When asked for the characteristics they would associate with their ideal 21st century school, their responses were enlightening. Taken together, they form a vision of a school that promotes active learning, democratic participation and a combination of individual creativity and collective responsibility:

> Teachers that take note of your opinions and things. *William, P7 boy*

> When you're not afraid to stand up in front of the class and tell about your ideas ... if you have an idea, people will listen to you. *Julie, P7 girl*

> If you're allowed to come up with ideas. I want to design cars, so I need to come up with new ideas. *Michael, P6 boy*

> A fair school – if people are different, you don't make fun of them. *Eilidh, P7 girl*

Much can be learned from pupils like these about the way in which enterprise and citizenship education should come together and promote pupil motivation and learning. It is time we started listening to them.

Summary

This final chapter has identified the main barriers to the full expression of citizenship and enterprise education as being the persistence of neo-liberal and neo-capitalist agendas. I have examined recent legislation and curriculum reform and made some predictions about the extent to which this will enable a maximal model to prevail in both England and Scotland. These predictions can be summarised as follows:

- In England the flexible framework of learning outcomes for citizenship education includes a focus on communitarian principles with opportunities for pupil-led agendas which combine economic dynamism and social justice. However, new legislation emerging from Westminster looks set to strengthen the authoritarian model of teaching and there is evidence to suggest that teachers are still hostile towards citizenship, enterprise and democratic learning.

- Curriculum reform in Scotland is creating new opportunities for promoting democratic values in schools, allowing more space for pupils to discuss issues and to engage in a progressive approach towards citizenship and enterprise. However, some critics feel that the tone of the new proposals promotes a focus on standards and targets and that plans to introduce new basic skills tests may undermine the Curriculum Review Group's vision.

Lawton (2005: 165) suggests a 'fourth way' for the British Labour party by which schools can become better, more humane places for educating children, free from the domination of neo-liberal and neo-capitalist agendas. Those of us who are committed to the principles associated with citizenship, enterprise and learning all hope that this vision becomes a reality in our lifetime.

Pause for reflection

What are your predictions about the future implementation of citizenship and enterprise education? Do you believe that schools will reach a point where they are genuinely democratic in their organisation and where pupils are encouraged to become active, responsible and enterprising citizens in the fullest sense? Take a few minutes to think about the characteristics you would associate with your ideal 21st century school and to estimate how far we are from achieving the model you describe.

Postscript
A pupil-led conference on
entrepreneurship

Ten years before this book was written, I implemented a business enterprise project while I was a primary 7 teacher in a school in East Dunbartonshire, just outside Glasgow. When I returned to the school to work with the P7 pupils of 2006, a great deal had changed in the wider enterprise education agenda: the debates about the role of social entrepreneurship had been combined with a national interest in education for citizenship. The two agendas of enterprise and citizenship can become infinitely more powerful when they are co-joined in educational policy and practice. The project subsequently carried out with the P7 pupils provides even more evidence that this is the case.

In the early stages of the project the children considered the qualities of enterprising people and jobs that could be carried out in an enterprising way, using a range of interactive materials and games. Through their discussion and debate the pupils came to realise that anyone can be enterprising, in any context, and that many of their concerns about local, national and global social issues could be addressed through creativity and enterprise. Through consultation with school staff the pupils decided to plan a mini-conference on entrepreneurship to raise awareness of the role of enterprise in addressing social problems.

Pupils formed themselves into groups to coordinate the conference publicity, ticket sales, programming, catering and audio-visual requirements. Two conference conveners and six team coordinators were appointed through interview and pupils chose to work either independently or in groups to design their conference papers. Each paper focused on a local, national or global social issue and pupils created their own enterprising solutions to the issues.

On the evening of the 'Enter Entrepreneurs' conference pupils presented their powerpoint presentations to their parents and staff members in the school. The content was wide and varied; while some pupils talked about issues such as the growing litter problem in Glasgow and the global effects of pollution, others talked about their views on teenage crime and drug abuse. Their solutions to these problems were at times both creative and controversial: while some proposed higher fines for dropping litter and curfews for the perpetrators of youth crime, others suggested the provision of more leisure activities for young people and for purpose-built graffiti walls to prevent the wider spread of this problem in residential areas.

Other groups of pupils chose to focus their research on the achievements of modern entrepreneurs. Some focused on the work of Bill Gates and Alan Sugar while others carried out research and design work on the Falkirk Wheel in Scotland as a feat of modern entrepreneurial engineering. One pupil, intensely moved by the plight of the street children in Kenya, chose to carry out research into how these children used basic materials to make toys, bags, clothes and other artefacts to make money to feed themselves. The pupils later decided to donate the money they had raised from their conference towards this African cause.

Planning this conference enabled the pupils to explore their understanding of contemporary local and global issues and the opportunities for enacting social change through enterprise. This new, informed knowledge was later used as the basis for them to begin the daunting task of writing the introduction to the school's enterprise policy statement, illustrated overleaf. In doing this they stated their view of enterprise education as a means of enabling other children to work towards finding creative solutions to different world issues. This democratic approach to policy development means that these pupils have left a legacy to guide the learning experiences of future generations of school pupils.

A pupil-led school policy on enterprise education

Introduction

At this school we understand the importance of enterprise topics in our curriculum. Children are encouraged to take part in as many elements of enterprise education as possible, through the pupil council, eco-schools committee and many other activities. Various aspects of school life are to do with enterprise education.

Objectives

By the end of P7 the pupils will be able to:

- Take part in various enterprise activities.

- Have knowledge of current affairs around the world and work towards enterprising solutions to social issues.

- Use skills such as problem solving, computing and working well in groups.

- Pick up skills from previous enterprise topics.

- Be able to make decisions and choices independently and in groups.

- Distinguish between business enterprise and community service enterprise.

- Develop confidence in speaking to different audiences about various issues.

The pupils of P7
June 2006

There is no doubt that projects of this kind enable the realisation of the four capacity areas upon which the *Curriculum for Excellence* is based. The children's experiences were clearly enabling them to become successful learners, since they developed a passion for learning about new social issues and demonstrated creativity in seeking new ways of working towards resolving these issues. They were becoming more confident individuals through exploring their own social values and beliefs and communicating their views of the world to wider audiences. Their developing interest in and concern for local and global issues was enabling them to develop informed, ethical views of the world and fostering an aspiration to engage as responsible citizens: they were developing enterprising attitudes and a commitment to become effective contributors to wider society.

Talking to pupils throughout the project, it was interesting to note how their opinions about enterprise changed. Although initially convinced that enterprise was associated exclusively with business, by the end of the project the pupils believed that people can be enterprising in a range of social contexts through having good ideas and creativity. It was clear that the pupils' expectations for consultation in school increased as a result of the project; while pupils were enthusiastic about the way in which teachers took their ideas on board, they increasingly began to feel that pupil council members could do more to listen to the wider pupil voice. It seems that the democratic classroom ethos the children had become accustomed to while planning and organising the conference had given them higher expectations.

This was a nostaligic period for me, a time when I was able to go back to my roots and put my research findings into practice through a combined focus on citizenship and enterprise. Like all good conferences, this pupil-led one generated new ideas that helped to inform the policy making agenda. Future generations of pupils in this school will surely benefit from the wisdom of these pupils, who have reconciled the principles associated with enterprise, citizenship and democracy through their ground-breaking project and associated school policy.

The Enter Entrepreneurs Conference

Application Form

Job applying for: Conference Convenor (2) Technical/AV. coordinator

Skills: I am a born leader. I have good people skills. I work hard at all times and I work well under pressure. The majority of people trust me. I am a succeeder and I don't let people down. I am a responsible and organized person. I am confident talking to a large group of people. The most important skill which I have is keeping everyone organized, making sure everyone is having fun and listening to others veiws.

Any additional information to support your application (eg. previous experience, interests, hobbies)

I have experience of leadership as I have been a captain of a debate team. I am relied on to captain my basketball team. I am not afraid to express my veiws if a member of the team is not playing their role in the team.

References

Alderson, P. (2000) School students' views on school councils and daily life at school, *Children and Society*, 14(2): 121-134.

Ashton, E. and Watson, B. (1998) Values education: a fresh look at procedural neutrality, *Educational Studies*, 24 (2): 183-193.

Baginsky, M. and Hannam, D. (1999) *School Councils: The Views of Students and Teachers*. London: NSPCC.

Baker, M. (2006) *Blair vs Brown: what will change* (education). BBC News: http://news.bbc.co.uk/1/hi/uk_ politics/5326626.stm (accessed on 08/09/06)

Ball, C. (1984) Educating for enterprise: the overseas experience, in: A. G. Watts and P. Moran (eds), *Education for Enterprise*. Cambridge: CRAC Publications.

Barclay, A., Bowes, A., Ferguson, I., Sim, D., Valenti, M. with Fard, S., MacKintosh, S. (2003) *Asylum Seekers in Scotland*. http://www.scotland.gov.uk/library5 (accessed on 31/01/05).

BBC News (2003) *Million March Against Iraq War*. http://news.bbc.co.uk/1/hi/uk/2765041.stm (accessed on 03/04/06).

Billett, S. (2004) From your business to our business: industry and vocational education in Australia, *Oxford Review of Education*, 30(1): 13-35.

Boyte, H. (2003) Civic education and the new American patriotism post-9/11, *Cambridge Journal of Education*, 33 (1): 85-100.

Brownlow, L., Deuchar, R., Foster, M., Paterson, M., Weir, D. (2004) *The Educational and Economic Benefits of Enterprise in Education, Volumes 1-3*. Glasgow: University of Strathclyde.

Brownlow, L., Twiddle, B., Watt, D. (1998) *Go for Enterprise*. Glasgow: Centre For Enterprise Education.

Burke, C. and Grosvenor, I. (2003) *The School I'd Like: Children and Young People's Reflections on an Education for the 21st Century*. London: Routledge-Farmer.

Carr, D. (2003) Democracy and citizenship, in: J. Crowther, I. Martin, M. Shaw (eds), *Renewing Democracy in Scotland: An Educational Sourcebook*. Leicester: NIACE.

Chomsky, N. (1988) Towards a humanistic conception of education and work, in: D. Corson (ed), *Education for Work: Background to Policy and Curriculum*. Clevedon/Philadelphia: Multilingual Matters Ltd.

Claire, H. (ed) (2004) *Teaching Citizenship in Primary Schools*. Exeter: Learning Matters Ltd.

CNN (2003) *Cities Jammed in Worldwide Protest of War in Iraq*. http://edition.cnn.co,/2003/US/02/15/sprj.irq.protests.main (accessed on 27/03/06).

Cogan, J.J. and Derricott, R. (2000) *Citizenship for the 21st Century*. London: Kogan Page.

Corson, D. (1988) Introduction: the meaning and place of work, in: D. Corson (ed), *Education for Work: Background to Policy and Curriculum*. Clevedon/Philadelphia: Multilingual Matters Ltd.

Covell, K. and Howe, B. (2001) Moral education through the 3 Rs: rights, respect and responsibility, *Journal of Moral Education*, 30 (1): 29-41.

Crick, B. and Porter, A. (eds) (1978) *Political Education and Political Literacy*. London: Longman.

Cunningham, S. and Lavalette, M. (2004) 'Active citizens' or 'irresponsible truants'? School student strikes against the war, *Critical Social Policy*, 24 (2): 255-269.

Curriculum Review Group (2004) *A Curriculum for Excellence*. Edinburgh: Scottish Executive.

Davies, I. (2002) Education for a better world?, in: I. Davies, I. Gregory, N. McGuinn (eds), *Key Debates in Education*. London and New York: Continuum.

Davies, I. and Evans, M. (2002) Encouraging active citizenship, *Educational Review*, 54 (1): 69-78.

Davies, I., Evans, M., Reid, A. (2005) Globalising citizenship education? A critique of 'global education' and 'citizenship education', *British Journal of Educational Studies*, 58 (1): 66-89.

Davies, I., Fulop, M., Hutchings, M., Ross, A., Vari-Szilagyi, I. (2001) Enterprising citizens? Perceptions of citizenship education and enterprise education in England and Hungary, *Educational Review*, 53 (3): 261-269.

Davies, I., Gregory, I., Riley, S.C. (1999) *Good Citizenship and Educational Provision*. London: Falmer Press.

Davies, I. and Issitt, J. (2005) Reflections on citizenship education in Australia, Canada and England, *Comparative Education*, 41 (4): 389-410.

Denholm, A. (2006) 'Switched off' from school? Take your turn at running it, *The Herald*, 9 January: 8.

Department of Education and Employment (1997) *Excellence in Schools*. London: The Stationery Office.

Department for Education and Skills (DfES) (2002) *Citizenship at Key Stage 4*. http://www.standards.dfes.gov.uk (accessed on 12/06/02).

Department for Education and Skills (DfES) (2003) *21st Century Skills: Realising Our Potential (Individuals, Employers, Nation)*. London: DfES.

Department for Education and Skills (DfES) (2005) *Higher Standards, Better Schools for All*. London: DfES.

Department for Education and Skills (DfES) (2006) *The Education and Inspections Bill 2006*. London: DfES.

Deuchar, R. (2003) Preparing tomorrow's people: the new challenges of citizenship education for involving Scottish pupils and teachers in participative decision-making processes, *Scottish Educational Review*, 35 (1): 27-37.

Deuchar, R. (2004) Changing paradigms: the potential of enterprise education as an adequate vehicle for promoting and enhancing education for active and responsible citizenship: illustrations from a Scottish perspective, *Oxford Review of Education*, 30 (2): 223-239.

Deuchar, R. (2004a) Reconciling self-interest and ethics: the role of primary school pupil councils, *Scottish Educational Review*, 36 (2): 159-168.

Deuchar, R. (2005) Business and ethics should 'go hand in hand', *The Herald: Society*, 22 November: 8-9.

Deuchar (2005a) Pupils deserve all the rights of citizenship, The Herald: Society, 19 April: 7-8.

Deuchar, R. (2005b) Summit of ambition must reach higher, *Times Educational Supplement Scotland*, 15 July: 18.

Deuchar (2006) Not only this, but also that! Translating the social and political motivations underpinning enterprise and citizenship education into Scottish schools, *Cambridge Review of Education*, 36 (4): 533-547.

Dewey, J. (1915) *School and Society*. Chicago: University of Chicago Press.

Dewey, J. (1938) *Experience and Education*. New York: MacMillan.

Dobie, T. (1998) Pupil councils in primary and secondary schools, in: D. Christie, H. Maitles, J. Halliday (eds), *Values Education for Democracy and Citizenship*. Glasgow: Gordon Cook Foundation/University of Strathclyde.

DuGay, P. (1991) Enterprise culture and the ideology of excellence, *New Formations*, 13: 45-61.

Durham University Business School (DUBS) (1988) *Enterprise: An Educational Resource for 14-19 Year Olds*. Durham: DUBS.

Fairclough, N. (2000) *New Labour, New Language?* London and New York: Routledge.

Faulks, K. (1998) *Citizenship in Modern Britain*. Edinburgh: University Press.

Faulks, K. (2000) *Citizenship*. London and New York: Routledge.

Fishman, S. M. and McCarthy, L. (1998) *John Dewey and the Challenge of Classroom Practice*. New York: Teachers College Press.

Flutter, J. and Ruddock, J. (2004) *Consulting the Pupils: What's In It for Schools?* London and New York: RoutledgeFalmer.

Forrester, K. (2003) Leaving the academic towers: the Council of Europe and the education for democratic citizenship project, *International Journal of Lifelong Education*, 22 (3): 221-234.

Fouts, J.T. and Chan, J.C.K. (1997) The development of work-study and school enterprises in China's schools, *Journal of Curriculum Studies*, 29 (1): 31-46.

Fraser, D. (2006) McConnell plan to have pupils sit basic literacy and numeracy tests, *The Herald*, 2 September: 6.

Gardner, H., Csikszentmihalyi, M., Damon, W. (2001) *Good Work: When Excellence and Ethics Meet*. USA: Basic Books.

121

Giddens, A. (1998) *The Third Way.* Cambridge: Polity Press.

Giddens, A. (2000) *The Third Way and its Critics.* Cambridge: Polity Press.

Goggin, P. (2003) Sharing values with a selfish gene, in: J. Gardner, J., J. Cairn, D. Lawton (eds), *Education for Values: Morals, Ethics and Citizenship in Contemporary Teaching.* London: Kogan Page Ltd.

Graves, J.B. (2005) *Cultural Democracy: The Arts, Community and the Public Purpose.* Urban and Chicago: University of Illinois Press.

Gregory, K. K. (1999) Impact of Enterprise Education on the Knowledge, Skills and Attitudes of Upper School Children? Unpublished MPhil thesis, University of Strathclyde.

Halstead, J. M. and Taylor, M. (2000) *The Development of Values, Attitudes and Personal Qualities: A Review of Recent Research.* Slough: NFER.

Hannam, D. (1998) Democratic education and education for democracy through pupil/student participation in decision making in schools, in: D. Christie, H. Maitles, J. Halliday (eds), *Values Education for Democracy and Citizenship.* Glasgow: Gordon Cook Foundation/University of Strathclyde.

Harber, C. (ed) (1995) *Developing Democratic Education.* Derby: Education Now.

Harber, C, (ed) (1998) *Voices for Democracy: A North-South Dialogue on Education for Sustainable Democracy.* Nottingham: Education Now Books.

Harber, C. (2004) *Schooling as Violence: How Schools Harm Pupils and Societies.* London: RoutledgeFalmer.

Hart, R. A. (1997) *Children's Participation: The Theory and Practice of Involving Young Citizens in Community Development and Environmental Care.* London: Earthscan Publications Ltd.

Hayward, G. (2004) A century of vocationalism, *Oxford Review of Education,* 30 (1): 3-12.

Heater, D. (1999) *What is Citizenship?* Cambridge: Polity Press.

Held, D. (2001) *Violence and Justice in a Global Age,* 14 September. http://www.opendemocracy.net (accessed on 05/04/06).

Her Majesty's Inspectors of Education (HMIE) (2004) *Quality Indicators in Enterprise in Education.* Edinburgh: HMIE.

Her Majesty's Inspectors of Education (HMIE) (2006) *Education for Citizenship: A Portrait of Current practice in Scottish Schools and Pre-School Centres.* Edinburgh: HMIE.

Holt (1987) *Skills and Vocationalism: The Easy Answer.* Milton Keyes: Open University Press.

Hunter, T. (2003) The great enabler brings satisfaction, *Times Educational Supplement Scotland,* 12 December: 22.

Hyland, T. (1991) Citizenship education and the enterprise culture, *Forum for the Discussion of New Trends in Education,* 33 (3): 86-88.

Ireland, N.(1993) Enterprise education in primary schools: a survey in two northern LEAs, *Education and Training,* 35 (4): 22-29.

Jamieson, I., Miller, A., Watts, A.G. (1988) *Mirrors of Work: Work Simulations in Schools.* London: Falmer Press.

Kearney, P. and Russell-Green, J. (1991) *Youth, Employment and Enterprise.* North Hobart: Enterprise Design Associates.

Kerr, D. (1999) Changing the political culture: the advisory group on education for citizenship and the teaching of democracy in schools, *Oxford Review of Education,* 25 (1-2): 275-284.

Kerr, D. (2004) *Changing the Political Culture: Reviewing the Progress of the Citizenship Education Initiative in England.* London: NFER.

Lasch, C. (1995) *The Revolt of the Elites.* New York: Norton.

Law, B. (1983) The colour-coded curriculum, *NICEC Training and Development Bulletin,* 23: 1-12.

Lawson, H. (2001) Active citizenship in schools and the community, *Curriculum Journal,* 12 (2): 163-178.

Lawton, D. (2005) *Education and Labour Party Ideologies 1900-2001.* London: RoutledgeFalmer.

Learning and Teaching Scotland (LTScotland) (2002) *Education for Citizenship in Scotland – A Paper for Discussion and Development.* Dundee: LT Scotland.

Loxley, A. and Thomas, G. (2001) Neo-conservatives, neo-liberals, the new left and inclusion: stirring the pot, *Cambridge Journal of Education,* 31 (3): 291-301.

Lynch, D. (1992) Can There Be a Progression Model for Enterprise Education? Unpublished MPhil thesis, Jordanhill College of Education.

MacDonald, R. (1991) Risky business? Youth and the enterprise culture, *Journal of Educational Policy,* 6 (3): 255-269.

Maitles, H. (2005) *Values in Education – We're All Citizens Now.* Edinburgh: Dunedin Academic Press.

Maitles, H. and Deuchar, R. (2004) '*I just don't like the whole thing about war!':* *Encouraging the Expression of Political Literacy among Primary Pupils as a Vehicle for Promoting Education for Active Citizenship.* http://www.leedsac.uk/ educol (accessed on 14/12/04).

Maitles, H. and Deuchar, R. (2004a) Why are they bombing innocent Iraqis? Encouraging the expression of political literacy among primary pupils as a vehicle for promoting education for active citizenship, *Improving Schools,* 7 (1): 97-105.

Maitles, H. and Gilchrist, I. (2003) *Never Too Young to Learn Democracy!: A Case Study of a Democratic Approach to Learning in an RME Secondary Class in the West of Scotland.* http://www.leedsac.uk/educol (accessed on 24/01/05).

Marshall, T.H. (1950) *Citizenship and Social Class and Other Essays.* Cambridge: Cambridge University Press.

Matseleng Allais, S. (2003) The National Qualifications Framework in South Africa: a democratic project trapped in a neo-liberal paradigm?, *Journal of Education and Work,* 16 (3): 305-324.

Mills, I. (2002) Research into Pupil Participation in Decision-Making. Unpublished conference paper, Scottish Educational Research Association (SERA), Westpark Conference Centre, Dundee: 26-28 September 2002.

123

National Curriculum Online (2006) *Citizenship at Key Stages 1-2*. http://www. nc.uk.net (accessed on 01/03/06).

Nicol, I. (2000) *Education for Work: A New Paradigm in Scottish Education?* Glasgow: National Centre for Education For Work.

OECD/CERI (1989) Towards an enterprising culture: a challenge to education and training, *Educational Monograph* 4: Paris.

Oliver, D. and Heater, D. (1994) *The Foundations of Citizenship*. New York: Harvester Wheatsheaf.

Osler, A. (2005) Education for democratic citizenship: new challenges in a globalised world, in: A. Osler and H. Starkey (eds), *Citizenship and Language Learning*. Stoke on Trent: Trentham.

Osler, A. and Starkey, H. (2001) Citizenship education and national identities in France and England: inclusive or exclusive?, *Oxford Review Of Education*, 27 (2): 287-303.

Osler, A. and Starkey, H. (2002) *Teacher Education and Human Rights*. London: David Fulton.

Peters, M. (1992) Starship education: enterprise culture in New Zealand, *Access: Critical Perspectives on Educational Policy*, 11 (1): 1-12.

Phipps, C. (2003) Children of the revolution: who can blame the decision-makers of the future for taking to the streets?, *The Guardian*, 22 March: 20.

Potter, J. (2002) *Active Citizenship in Schools*. London: Kogan Page Ltd.

Qualifications and Curriculum Authority (QCA) (1998) *Education for Citizenship and the Teaching of Democracy in Schools*. London: QCA.

Respect Task Force (2006) *Respect Action Plan*. http://www.respect.gov.uk/ assets/docs/respect_action_plan.pdf (accessed on 20/03/06).

Richardson, R. (1996) The terrestrial teacher, in: M.Steiner (ed), *Developing the Global Teacher*. Stoke-On-Trent: Trentham.

Ritchie, J. (1991) Chasing shadows: enterprise culture as an educational phenomenon, *Journal of Educational Policy*, 6 (3): 315-325.

Rowe, D. (2000) The words don't fit the music, *Tomorrow's Citizen*, Summer 2000: 25-26.

Ruddock, J. and Flutter, J. (2004) *How To Improve Your School*. London: Continuum.

Ryan, P. (2003) Evaluating vocationalism, *European Journal of Education*, 38 (2): 147-162.

Schwarz, W. (1989) *The New Dissenters: The Non-Conformist Conscience in the Age of Thatcher*. London: Bedford Square Press.

Schweisfurth, M. (2006) Education for global citizenship: teacher agency and curricular structure in Ontario schools, *Educational Review*, 58 (1): 41-50.

Scottish Education Department (SED) (1963) *From School to Further Education: Report of a Working Party on the Linkage of Secondary and Further Education*. Edinburgh: HMSO.

Scottish Executive (2001) *A Smart Successful Scotland: Ambitions for the Enterprise Networks*. http://www.scotland.gov.uk/library3/enterprise/sss-00.asp (accessed on 13/12/04).

Scottish Executive (2001a) *Better Behaviour – Better Learning: Report of the Discipline Task Group*. Edinburgh: SEED.

Scottish Executive (2002) *Determined to Succeed*. Edinburgh: SEED.

Scottish Executive (2003) *Life through Learning; Learning through Life*. Edinburgh: SEED.

Scottish Executive (2003a) *Ministerial Response to 'Determined to Succeed'*. http:// www.scotland.gov.uk (accessed on 06/04/04).

Scottish Executive (2004) *Determined to Succeed – One Year On*. Edinburgh: SEED.

Scottish Executive (2005) *Assessment is for Learning: Information Sheet*. Scotland: Scottish Executive/LTScotland/SQA.

Shacklock, G., Hattam, R., Smyth, J. (2000) Enterprise education and teachers' work: exploring the links, *Journal of Education and Work*, 13 (1): 41-58.

Shallcross, T., Robinson, J., Pace, P., Wals, A. (eds) (2006) *Creating Sustainable Environments in our Schools*. Stoke on Trent: Trentham.

Shilling, C. (1989) *Schooling for Work in Capitalist Britain*. New York/ Philadelphia/London: Falmer Press.

Shuttleworth, D. E. (1993) *Enterprise Learning in Action: Education and Economic Renewal for the 21st Century*. London: Routledge.

Smith, I. (2006) Excellence is not the only ambition, *Times Educational Supplement Scotland*, 31 March: 20.

Smyth, J. (1999) Schooling and enterprise culture: pause for a critical policy analysis, *Journal of Education Policy*, 14 (4): 435-444.

Starkey, H. (2005) Language teaching for democratic citizenship, in: A. Osler and H. Starkey (eds), *Citizenship Education and Language Learning*. Stoke on Trent: Trentham.

Taylor, A. (2005) 'Re-culturing' students and selling futures: school to work policy in Ontario, *Journal of Education and Work*, 18 (3): 321-340.

Taylor, M.J. and Johnson, R. (2002) *School Councils: Their Role in Citizenship and Personal and Social Education*. Berkshire: NFER.

Totterdell, M. (2000) The moralization of teaching: a relational approach as an ethical framework in the professional preparation and formation of teachers, in: R. Gardner, J. Cairns, D. Lawton (eds), *Education for Values*. London/Sterling: VA: Kogan Page.

United Nations General Assembly (1989) *Convention on the Rights of the Child*. http://www.cirp.org/ library/ethics/UN-convention (accessed on 16/03/06).

United Nations Sustainable Development (1992) *Agenda 21*. http://www.un. org.esa.sustdev/documents/agenda21 (accessed on 31/03/06).

Waiton, S. (2001) *Scared of the Kids? Curfews, Crime and the Regulation of Young People*. Sheffield: Sheffield Hallam University Press.

Waiton, S. (2006) *Anti-Social Behaviour: The Construction of a Crime*, 19 January. http://www.spiked-online.co.uk/Articles/0000000CAF28.htm (accessed on 05/04/06).

Watts, A.G. (1984) Education for enterprise: the concept and the context, in: A. G. Watts and P. Moran (eds), *Education for Enterprise*. Cambridge: CRAC Publications.

Weir, A. D. (1988) *Professional Issues in Education Number 4: Education and Vocation 14-18*. Edinburgh: Scottish Academic Press.

White, P. (1999) Political education in the early years: the place of civic values, *Oxford Review of Education*, 25 (1-2): 59-69.

Wilkins, C. (2001) Student teachers and attitudes towards 'race': the role of citizenship education in addressing racism through the curriculum, *Westminster Studies In Education*, 24 (1): 7-21.

Young Enterprise (2006) *Key Stage 2*. http://www.young-enterprise.org.uk (accessed on 01/03/06).

Index